Blue Pastures

Mary Oliver

Blue Pastures

Mariner Books
An Imprint of HarperCollins *Publishers*
Boston   New York

Mariner Books
An Imprint of HarperCollins Publishers, registered in the United States
of America and/or other jurisdictions.

www.marinerbooks.com

Excerpt from "Anatomy of Death." From *The Flowering Stone* by
George Dillon (Viking, 1931). Copyright © 1931 by George Dillon.
Copyright renewed 1959 by George Dillon. Reprinted courtesy of
Nan Sherman Sussmann.

"Archaic Torso of Apollo" by Rainer Maria Rilke. From *Selected
Poems of Rainer Maria Rilke,* edited and translated by Robert Bly.
Copyright © 1981 by Robert Bly. Reprinted by permission of
HarperCollins Publishers, Inc.

Library of Congress Cataloging-in-Publication Data
Oliver, Mary, 1935–
Blue pastures/Mary Oliver.
p. cm.
"A Harvest Original"
ISBN 0-15-100190-1.—ISBN 0-15-600215-9 (pbk.)
I. Title.
PS3565.L5B57 1995
814'.54—dc20 95-16881

Designed by Lydia D'moch

First edition

ScoutAutomatedPrintCode

Publication acknowledgments appear on pages 121 - 22, which
constitute a continuation of the copyright page.

For Molly Malone Cook

Contents

Blue Pastures

Of Power and Time

It is a silver morning like any other. I am at my desk.
Then the phone rings, or someone raps at the door. I
am deep in the machinery of my wits. Reluctantly I
rise, I answer the phone or I open the door. And the
thought which I had in hand, or almost in hand, is
gone.

Creative work needs solitude. It needs concentration, without interruptions. It needs the whole sky to
fly in, and no eye watching until it comes to that certainty which it aspires to, but does not necessarily have
at once. Privacy, then. A place apart—to pace, to chew
pencils, to scribble and erase and scribble again.

But just as often, if not more often, the interruption comes not from another but from the self itself,
or some other self within the self, that whistles and
pounds upon the door panels and tosses itself, splashing, into the pond of meditation. And what does it
have to say? That you must phone the dentist, that
you are out of mustard, that your uncle Stanley's birth-
day is two weeks hence. You react, of course. Then
you return to your work, only to find that the imps of
idea have fled back into the mist.

It is this internal force—this intimate interrupter—whose tracks I would follow. The world sheds, in the energetic way of an open and communal place, its many greetings, as a world should. What quarrel can there be with that? But that the self can interrupt the self—and does—is a darker and more curious matter.

I am, myself, three selves at least. To begin with, there is the child I was. Certainly I am not that child anymore! Yet, distantly, or sometimes not so distantly, I can hear that child's voice—I can feel its hope, or its distress. It has not vanished. Powerful, egotistical, insinuating—its presence rises, in memory, or from the steamy river of dreams. It is not gone, not by a long shot. It is with me in the present hour. It will be with me in the grave.

And there is the attentive, social self. This is the smiler and the doorkeeper. This is the portion that winds the clock, that steers through the dailiness of life, that keeps in mind appointments that must be made, and then met. It is fettered to a thousand notions of obligation. It moves across the hours of the day as though the movement itself were the whole task. Whether it gathers as it goes some branch of wisdom or delight, or nothing at all, is a matter with which it is hardly concerned. What this self hears night and day, what it loves beyond all other songs, is the endless springing forward of the clock, those measures strict and vivacious, and full of certainty.

The clock! That twelve-figured moon skull, that

white spider belly! How serenely the hands move with their filigree pointers, and how steadily! Twelve hours, and twelve hours, and begin again! Eat, speak, sleep, cross a street, wash a dish! The clock is still ticking. All its vistas are just so broad—are *regular.* (Notice that word.) Every day, twelve little bins in which to order disorderly life, and even more disorderly thought. The town's clock cries out, and the face on every wrist hums or shines; the world keeps pace with itself. Another day is passing, a regular and *ordinary* day. (Notice that word also.)

Say you have bought a ticket on an airplane and you intend to fly from New York to San Francisco. What do you ask of the pilot when you climb aboard and take your seat next to the little window, which you cannot open but through which you see the dizzying heights to which you are lifted from the secure and friendly earth?

Most assuredly you want the pilot to be his regular and ordinary self. You want him to approach and undertake his work with no more than a calm pleasure. You want nothing fancy, nothing new. You ask him to do, routinely, what he knows how to do—fly an airplane. You hope he will not daydream. You hope he will not drift into some interesting meander of thought. You want this flight to be ordinary, not extraordinary. So, too, with the surgeon, and the ambulance driver, and the captain of the ship. Let all of them work, as ordinarily they do, in confident familiarity with whatever the work requires, and no more. Their ordinariness is the surety of the world. Their ordinariness makes the world go round.

I, too, live in this ordinary world. I was born into it. Indeed, most of my education was intended to make me feel comfortable within it. Why that enterprise failed is another story. Such failures happen, and then, like all things, are turned to the world's benefit, for the world has a need of dreamers as well as shoemakers. (Not that it is so simple, in fact—for what shoemaker does not occasionally thump his thumb when his thoughts have, as we would say, "wandered"? And when the old animal body clamors for attention, what daydreamer does not now and again have to step down from the daydream and hurry to market before it closes, or else go hungry?)

And this is also true. In creative work—creative work *of all kinds*—those who are the world's working artists are not trying to help the world go around, but forward. Which is something altogether different from the ordinary. Such work does not refute the ordinary. It is, simply, something else. Its labor requires a different outlook—a different set of priorities. Certainly there is within each of us a self that is neither a child, nor a servant of the hours. It is a third self, occasional in some of us, tyrant in others. This self is out of love with the ordinary; it is out of love with time. It has a hunger for eternity.

Intellectual work sometimes, spiritual work certainly, artistic work always—these are forces that fall within its grasp, forces that must travel beyond the realm of the hour and the restraint of the habit. Nor can the actual work be well separated from the entire life. Like the knights of the middle ages, there is little the creatively inclined person can do but to prepare himself, body and spirit, for the labor to come—for his adventures are all unknown. In truth, the work itself is the adventure. And no artist could go about this work, or would want to, with less than extraordinary energy and concentration. The extraordinary is what art is about.

Neither is it possible to control, or regulate, the machinery of creativity. One must work with the creative powers—for not to work with is to work against; in art as in spiritual life there is no neutral place. Especially at the beginning, there is a need of discipline as well as solitude and concentration. A writing schedule is a good suggestion to make to young writers, for example. Also, it is enough to tell them. Would one tell them so soon the whole truth, that one must be ready at all hours, and always, that the ideas in their shimmering forms, in spite of all our conscious discipline, will come when they will, and on the swift upheaval of their wings—disorderly; reckless; as unmanageable, sometimes, as passion.

No one yet has made a list of places where the extraordinary may happen and where it may not. Still, there are indications. Among crowds, in drawing rooms, among easements and comforts and pleasures, it is seldom seen. It likes the out-of-doors. It likes the concentrating mind. It likes solitude. It is more likely to stick to the risk-taker than the ticket-taker. It isn't that it would disparage comforts, or the set routines of the world, but that its concern is directed to another place. Its concern is the edge, and the making of a form out of the formlessness that is beyond the edge.

Of this there can be no question—creative work requires a loyalty as complete as the loyalty of water to the force of gravity. A person trudging through the wilderness of creation who does not know this—who does not swallow this—is lost. He who does not crave that roofless place *eternity* should stay at home. Such a person is perfectly worthy, and useful, and even beautiful, but is not an artist. Such a person had better live with timely ambitions and finished work formed for the sparkle of the moment only. Such a person had better go off and fly an airplane.

There is a notion that creative people are absent-minded, reckless, heedless of social customs and obligations. It is, hopefully, true. For they are in another world altogether. It is a world where the third self is governor. Neither is the purity of art the innocence of childhood, if there is such a thing. One's life as a child, with all its emotional rages and ranges, is but grass for the winged horse—it must be chewed well in those savage teeth. There are irreconcilable differences between acknowledging and examining the fabulations of one's past and dressing them up as though they were adult figures, fit for art, which they never will be. The working, concentrating artist is an adult who refuses interruption from himself, who remains absorbed and energized in and by the work—who is thus responsible to the work.

On any morning or afternoon, serious interruptions to work, therefore, are never the inopportune, cheerful, even loving interruptions which come to us from another. Serious interruptions come from the watchful eye we cast upon ourselves. There is the blow that knocks the arrow from its mark! There is the drag we throw over our own intentions. There is the interruption to be feared!

It is six A.M., and I am working. I am absent-minded, reckless, heedless of social obligations, etc. It is as it must be. The tire goes flat, the tooth falls out, there will be a hundred meals without mustard. The poem gets written. I have wrestled with the angel and I am stained with light and I have no shame. Neither do I have guilt. My responsibility is not to the ordinary, or the timely. It does not include mustard, or teeth. It does not extend to the lost button, or the beans in the pot. My loyalty is to the inner vision, whenever and howsoever it may arrive. If I have a meeting with you at three o'clock, rejoice if I am late. Rejoice even more if I do not arrive at all.

There is no other way work of artistic worth can be done. And the occasional success, to the striver, is worth everything. The most regretful people on earth are those who felt the call to creative work, who felt their own creative power restive and uprising, and gave to it neither power nor time.

At Herring Cove

The edge of the sea shines and glimmers. The tide rises and falls, on ordinary not on stormy days, about nine feet. The beach here is composed of sand and glacial drift; the many-colored pebbles of this drift have been well rounded by the water's unceasing, manipulative, glassy touch. In addition, all sorts of objects are carried here by the currents, by the galloping waves, and left as the sea on the outgoing tide tumbles back.

From one tide to the next, and from one year to the next, what do I find here?

Grapefruit, and orange peel, and onion sacks from the fishing boats; balloons of all colors, with ribbons dangling; beer cans, soft drink cans, plastic bags, plastic bottles, plastic bottle caps, feminine hygiene by-products, a few summers ago several hypodermic needles, the odd glove and the odd shoe, plastic glasses, old cigarette lighters, mustard bottles, plastic containers still holding the decomposing bodies of baitfish; fishhooks rusty or still shining, coils of fishline; balls of fishline, one with a razor-billed auk in death-grip.

Sea clams, razor clams, mussels holding on with their long beards to stones or each other; a very occasional old oyster and quahog shell; other shells in varying degrees of whiteness: drills, whelks, jingles, slippers, periwinkles, moon snails. Bones of fish, bodies of fish and of skates, pipefish, goosefish, jellyfish, dogfish, starfish, sand dabs; blues or parts of blues or the pink, satiny guts of blues; sand eels in the blackened seaweed, silver, and spackled with salt.

Dead harbor seal, dead gull, dead merganser, dead gannet with tiny ivory-colored lice crawling over its snowy head and around its aster-blue eyes. Dead dovekie in winter.

Once, on a summer morning at exact low tide, the skull of a dolphin at the edge of the water. Later the flanged backbone, tail bones, hip bones slide onto the sand and return no more to the gardens of the sea.

One set of car keys. One quarter, green and salt-pocked.

Egg case of the left-handed whelk, black egg cases of skates; sea lace, the sandy nests of the moon snail, not one without its break in the circle; once, after a windy night, a drenched sea mouse.

More gorgeous than anything the mind of man has yet or ever will imagine, a moth, *Hyalophora cecropia,* in the first morning of its long death. I think of Thoreau's description of one he found in the Concord woods: "it looked like a young emperor just donning the most splendid robes that ever emperor wore...." The wings are six inches across, and no part of them

is without an extraordinary elaboration of design—
swirls, circles, and lines, brief and shaped like lightning. Upon its taut understructure, the wings are pow-
dery and hairy, like the finest fur closely shorn. White
and cream and black, and a silver-blue, wine red and
rust red, a light brown here and a darker brown there
and still a deeper brown elsewhere, not to speak of the
snowy white of the body's cylinder, and the stripes of
the body, and the red fringe of the body, and the rust-
colored legs, and the black plumes of the antennae.
Once it was the hungry green worm. Then it flew,
through the bottleneck of the deepest sleep, through
the nets of the wind, into the warm field. And now it
is the bright trash of the past, its emptiness perfect,
and terrible.

My Friend Walt Whitman

In Ohio, in the 1950s, I had a few friends who kept me sane, alert, and loyal to my own best and wildest inclinations. My town was no more or less congenial to the fact of poetry than any other small town in America—I make no special case of a solitary childhood. Estrangement from the mainstream of that time and place was an unavoidable precondition, no doubt, to the life I was choosing from among all the lives possible to me.

I never met any of my friends, of course, in a usual way—they were strangers, and lived only in their writings. But if they were only shadow-companions, still they were constant, and powerful, and amazing. That is, they said amazing things, and for me it changed the world.

This hour I tell things in confidence,
I might not tell everybody but I will tell you.

Whitman was the brother I did not have. I did have an uncle, whom I loved, but he killed himself one rainy fall day; Whitman remained, perhaps more avuncular for the loss of the other. He was the gypsy boy my sister and I went off with into the far fields beyond the town, with our pony, to gather strawberries. The boy from Romania moved away; Whitman shone on in the twilight of my room, which was growing busy with books, and notebooks, and muddy boots, and my grandfather's old Underwood typewriter.

> *My voice goes after what my eyes cannot reach,*
> *With the twirl of my tongue I encompass worlds and*
>   *volumes of worlds.*

When the high school I went to experienced a crisis of delinquent student behavior, my response was to start out for school every morning but to turn most mornings into the woods instead, with a knapsack of books. Always Whitman's was among them. My truancy was extreme, and my parents were warned that I might not graduate. For whatever reason, they let me continue to go my own way. It was an odd blessing, but a blessing all the same. Down by the creek, or in the wide pastures I could still find on the other side of the deep woods, I spent my time with my friend: my brother, my uncle, my best teacher.

> *The moth and the fisheggs are in their place,*
> *The suns I see and the suns I cannot see are in their place,*

> *The palpable is in its place and the impalpable is in its place.*

Thus Whitman's poems stood before me like a model of delivery when I began to write poems myself: I mean the oceanic power and rumble that travels through a Whitman poem—the incantatory syntax, the boundless affirmation. In those years, truth was elusive—as was my own faith that I could recognize and contain it. Whitman kept me from the swamps of a worse uncertainty, and I lived many hours within the lit circle of his certainty, and his bravado. *Unscrew the locks from the doors! Unscrew the doors themselves from their jambs!* And there was the passion which he invested in the poems. The metaphysical curiosity! The oracular tenderness with which he viewed the world—its roughness, its differences, the stars, the spider—nothing was outside the range of his interest. I reveled in the specificity of his words. And his faith— that kept my spirit buoyant surely, though his faith was without a name that I ever heard of. *Do you guess I have some intricate purpose? Well I have . . . for the April rain has, and the mica on the side of a rock has.*

But first and foremost, I learned from Whitman that the poem is a temple—or a green field—a place to enter, and in which to feel. Only in a secondary way is it an intellectual thing—an artifact, a moment of seemly and robust wordiness—wonderful as that part of it is. I learned that the poem was made not just to exist, but to speak—to be company. It was everything

that was needed, when everything was needed. I remember the delicate, rumpled way into the woods,
and the weight of the books in my pack. I remember
the rambling, and the loafing—the wonderful days
when, with Whitman, *I tucked my trowser-ends in my
boots and went and had a good time.*

Owls

Upon the dunes and in the shaggy woodlands of the Provincelands, I have seen plenty of owls. Heard them at twilight and in the dark, and near dawn. Watched them, flying over Great Pond, flying over Rose Tasha's noisy barnyard, flying out of the open fretwork of the spire of the old Methodist Church on Commercial Street, where the pigeons sleep, and disappear one by one. I have seen them in every part of the woods, favoring this or that acreage until the rabbits are scarce and they move to new hunting grounds, and then, in a few seasons, move back.

In January and February I walk in the woods and look for a large nest in a tall tree. In my mind's eye I see the great horned, the early nester, sitting upon her bulk of sticks, like an old woman on a raft.

I look in every part of the Provincelands that is within my walking range. I look by Clapps Pond and Bennet Pond and Round Pond and Oak-Head Pond. I look along the riding trail that borders the landfill—in the old days a likely hunting ground and not one disdained by the owls or much else. I look in the woods close to the airport, so often have I flushed an owl from the pine trees there.

And I look in the woods around Pasture Pond, where, over a century ago, Mr. George Washington Ready, once the Provincetown town crier, saw the six-eyed sea serpent. He witnessed it, he said, emerging from the ocean and slithering across the dunes. Into Pasture Pond it descended, and sank from sight. Every winter I stare into the ice of the pond and think of it—still asleep, I suppose, in the clasp of the lily roots, for no one has ever seen it again.

And I search in the deeper woods, past fire roads and the bike trail, among the black oaks and the taller pines, in the silent blue afternoons, when the sand is still frozen and the snow falls slowly and aimlessly, and the whole world smells like water in an iron cup. And I see, on my way to the owl's nest, many marvelous things: the gray hives of the paper wasps, hidden in summer by the leaves but now apparent on the boughs; nests, including one of the Baltimore oriole, with fishline woven into it, so that it has in the wind a comet's tail of rippling white threads; and pheasants, birds that were released into fall's russet fields but find themselves still alive at the far end of winter, and are glad of it, storming upward from the fields on their bright wings; and great blue herons, thin and melancholy; and deer, in their gray winter coats, bounding through the cold bogs; an owl in a tree with an unexpected face—a barred owl, seen once and once only.

Finally the earth grows softer, and the buds on the

trees swell, and the afternoon becomes a wider room to roam in, as the sun moves back from the south and the light grows stronger. The bluebirds come back, and the robins, and the song sparrows, and great robust flocks of blackbirds; and in the fields blackberry hoops put on a soft plum color, a restitution; the ice on the ponds begins to thunder, and between the slices is seen the strokes of its breaking up, a stutter of dark lightning. And then the winter is over, and again I have not found the great horned owl's nest.

But the owls themselves are not hard to find, silent and on the wing, with their ear tufts flat against their heads as they fly and their huge wings alternately gliding and flapping as they maneuver through the trees. Athena's owl of wisdom and Merlin's companion, Archimedes, were screech owls surely, not this bird with the glassy gaze, restless on the bough, nothing but blood on its mind.

When the great horned is in the trees its razor-tipped toes rasp the limb, flakes of bark fall through the air and land on my shoulders while I look up at it and listen to the heavy, crisp, breathy snapping of its hooked beak. The screech owl I can imagine on my wrist, also the delicate saw-whet that flies like a big soft moth down by Great Pond. And I can imagine sitting quietly before that luminous wanderer the snowy owl, and learning, from the white gleam of its feathers, something about the arctic. But the great horned I can't imagine in any such proximity—if one of those should touch me, it would touch to the center of my life, and I must fall. They are the pure wild hunters of our world. They are swift and merciless upon the backs of rabbits, mice, voles, snakes, even skunks, even cats sitting in dusky yards, thinking peaceful thoughts. I have found the headless bodies of rabbits and blue jays, and known it was the great horned owl that did them in, taking the head only, for the owl has an insatiable craving for the taste of brains. I have walked with prudent caution down paths at twilight when the dogs were puppies. I know this bird. If it could, it would eat the whole world.

In the night, when the owl is less than exquisitely swift and perfect, the scream of the rabbit is terrible. But the scream of the owl, which is not of pain and hopelessness and the fear of being plucked out of the world, but of the sheer rollicking glory of the death-bringer, is more terrible still. When I hear it resounding through the woods, and then the five black pellets of its song dropping like stones into the air, I know I am standing at the edge of the mystery, in which terror is naturally and abundantly part of life, part of even the most becalmed, intelligent, sunny life—as, for example, my own. The world where the owl is endlessly hungry and endlessly on the hunt is the world in which I live too. There is only one world.

Sometimes, while I have stood listening to the owl's song drifting through the trees, when it is ten degrees above nothing and life for any small creature is hard enough without *that,* I have found myself thinking of summer fields. Fields full of flowers—

poppies or lupines. Or, here, fields where the roses hook into the dunes, and their increase is manyfold. All summer they are red and pink and white tents of softness and nectar, which wafts and hangs everywhere—a sweetness so palpable and excessive that, before it, I'm struck, I'm taken, I'm conquered; I'm washed into it, as though it was a river, full of dreaming and idleness—I drop to the sand, I can't move; I am restless no more; I am replete, supine, finished, filled to the last edges with an immobilizing happiness. And is this not also terrible? Is this not also frightening?

Are the roses not also—even as the owl is—excessive? Each flower is small and lovely, but in their sheer and silent abundance the roses become an immutable force, as though the work of the wild roses was to make sure that all of us, who come wandering over the sand, may be, for a while, struck to the heart and saturated with a simple joy. Let the mind be teased by such *stretches* of the imagination, by such balance. Now I am cringing at the very sound of the owl's dark wings opening over my head—not long ago I could do nothing but lounge on the sand and stare into the cities of the roses.

I have two feathers from the big owl. One I found near Round Pond; the other, on another day, fell as I watched the bird rise from one tree and flap into another. As the owl rose, some crows caught sight of it, and so began another scrimmage in their long battle.

The owl wants to sleep, but the crows pursue it and when it settles a second time the crows—now a dozen—gather around and above it, and scream into its face, with open beaks and wagging tongues. They come dangerously close to its feet, which are huge and quick. The caught crow is a dead crow. But it is not in the nature of crows to hide or cower—it is in their nature to gather and to screech and to gamble in the very tree where death stares at them with molten eyes. What fun, to aggravate the old bomber! What joy, to swipe at the tawny feathers even as the bird puffs and hulks and hisses.

But finally the owl rises from the trees altogether and climbs and floats away, over two or three hills, and the crows go off to some other merriment.

And I walk on, over the shoulder of summer and down across the red-dappled fall; and, when it's late winter again, out through the far woodlands of the Provincelands, maybe another few hundred miles, looking for the owl's nest, yes, of course, and looking at everything else along the way.

Blue Pastures

M. and I steered our wooden boat with the ratcheting motor to the breakwater and a little beyond, threw out the anchor, and baited our hooks. All afternoon we drew in the trembling lines only to find the hooks clean, the bait taken. We put on more bait; we were without instruction and did not know how long it might take to catch something. Later, it was explained that we had been feeding crabs—calicos, probably, or some elated gathering of the greens. As far as fishing went, we used wrong bait and did not engage it to the hooks properly, we were in the wrong part of the harbor at the wrong time according to the tides, and so on.

We were rather glad. We meant, of course, to catch fish. Nevertheless, the hours passed pleasantly, and we found that we were content to have wrested no leaping form from the water. The fact that we caught nothing became, in fact, part of the pleasing aspect of the day. The water was deep and luminous and ever moving; the sky clean and distant; the mood more suitable for slow, long-limbed thoughts than for taking from even the simplest husk of body its final thimble of breath.

On the other hand, as I walk the beach, I have found fish that were hooked and gaffed somewhere nearby and then not quite drawn into the boat. So, they are mine. Some dissatisfied fisherman once left three pollack lying on the sand. I carried them home without compunction and made judicious use of their sweet and snowy bodies.

But whether one is part of the action or not, fishing is always one of the apparent vitalities here. The sea surrounds us. It surrounds the houses and the two long, occasionally bending streets. It surrounds idle conversation; it surrounds the mind diving down into what it hopes is original thought.

One summer morning, neighbors brought us a black duck that dogs had chased to exhaustion along the beach. She rested, and ate, and dozed on the cold floor of the shower. That summer there was, in our neighborhood, an old tomcat, stray—except that we had gotten into the habit of giving him supper, as well as occasional assistance for his sometimes ghastly wounds. At twilight, he would enter through the kitchen window, eat, wash, nap, and leave. When he entered and found the duck, his lean hips swung with surprise and malice. The duck froze. Then the moment broke: the duck prinked her feathers and slapped away to the shower; the cat went casually through his routine, then leaped back into summer night.

After a few days we carried the duck to the water's edge. She settled on the waves just at the brimming of the tide and paddled toward her flock, which was at rest near the breakwater. As she moved away we saw, like a black stitch in the water, something moving toward her, then past her, then straight toward us. It was the steep, dorsal fin of a shark. How can one understand such timing, what curious sense does it make, in all the happenings of the universe? In it came, close to the shore—an eight- or nine-foot blue shark. Then it turned—something was wrong—it wobbled a little. An eye, as big as a teacup, tipped toward us. The enormous fish hung in the water about the pilings of an unused and dilapidated wharf. Some young men on the shore also saw it, and came, sprinting, with two-by-fours and metal poles. I shouted— why would they hurt it? They paid no attention, and the shark slid away, and then returned again. I shouted a second time—I wrung my hands. The young men stared and grumbled, but they left the wharf. The shark turned and righted itself and boiled away, into the deeper water.

I have seen the bodies of bluefin tuna cleaned (field-dressed, it might be more proper to say), lying on the wharf, waiting for the winches to swing them into the packing plant. Their bodies are the size of horses— 700 pounds, 800 pounds. More often than not, they are flown to Japan for quick and expensive consumption. Thirty boats may gather off the coast when a bluefin tuna is caught, hoping for more. I saw one only once:

in the morning light, in the distance, a golden horse leaping in and out of the waves.

One afternoon I was aboard the whale-watching vessel the *Dolphin* when the big boat steamed past an ocean sunfish, an enormous bulbous affair, its head scarcely distinguishable from the blown body. It floated easily and without a sound; it could have been asleep.

The flounder makes a pretty supper. So does mackerel—a squamation of snow, midnight, and the blue of a stormy sky. The sea clam, when you clean it—when you cut the hoof from the center of the body—flinches back, the pink flesh tightens against the knife. Mussels open without a sound in the steam, but they make a curious sighing sound when you first reach for them on the rocks; perhaps the picker's shadow tells them, the darkness deepening, that their lives are almost over. Nothing tastes so good as the quahog, opened as soon as found, on the flats, in the cold gray light. You cut it loose from the filmy underpinning, slide it onto the tongue. The gulls know how it tastes. They see you do this and turn in midair. With a sudden skirl they drop, tuning their white feathers to swift descent, and stand about you on the sand, and their faces beg.

I have seen bluefish arc and sled across the water, an acre of them, leaping and sliding back under the water, then leaping again, toothy, terrible, lashed by hunger. The fish they are after, a blood-smeared cloud, are driven sometimes in their search for escape onto the very sand. Porgies, perhaps. With chunks missing from their bodies. Half bodies, still leaping.

Striped bass may be eighty pounds, a hundred pounds. I have never seen them in the sea, but I have seen them iced and boxed, or roped to the fishermen's trucks, like the bodies of deer.

Other fish I have seen by chance: cod, the mild whiting. Now and then a dead goosefish on the beach, all of it but the enormous gate of its mouth sagging under the hot sun. Once, a tautog. But, again, I remember that the fisherman in this case, who had hoped for something else, left it on the sand. Once, a sea robin, in a small boy's pail.

Squid occasionally beach themselves, sputtering and rolling in the swash. They take more time to clean than to gather. They taste like chicken, but are richer by far: the taste of five chickens in each tubular body.

Little skates are common. Fishermen dislike them, for they take the bait frequently, and break lines, and use up time, and flop dismally on the sand when released. I have seen fishermen standing on their wide, crenulated wings in order to rip back the hook that dragged the skate forth in the first place. I have seen few fishermen bother to slide them again into the water. They die, and gulls eat them, or the young eagles, when we are fortunate enough to be visited by those great, dark-feathered birds. The strange face of the skate is haunting, and perhaps it haunts the fishermen, too—the human-looking, spit-releasing mouth, and the sudden motion of the thick eyelids as they descend and rise again over the bulging, death-sick eyes. I hope so. Their soft, white bellyskin is plucked open in an hour by the rapacious beaks of the gulls. But their cartilage frames waste away slowly. Like small kites they drift on the tides to the upper beach, where they endure a long time.

Merciless, too, are the fishermen to the supple, black dogfish. One finds them, horribly gaffed, or hacked in half, floating out of the water.

But not every fisherman is so knife-quick. Once I was on a boat when a fisherman—a Provincetown man—hauled in an appalling-looking creature: an enormous spider crab, like an angel of desolation, with a domed body a foot across and nearly as high. The long limbs hung limp and were stuck with bits of seaweed and shells, water sluiced out of the vague centrality of its body, between its forelimbs the eyes gazed humbly. The body shell, too, was festooned with fragments of weed and flotsam. The spider crab dresses its body to make a camouflage, reaching back with a limb and daubing itself with whatever materials are lying about. The fisherman sighed and dropped the mess to the bottom of the boat. He knelt, and worked at the hook. "Never take from the sea what you don't use," he said, and stood up, and swung the crab over the gunnel.

And once, too, I gave something back. A friend left us a bluefish. I went down to the edge of the water to clean it. When I had it scaled and slipped the sharp knife into the bellyflesh, it broke open, not from any carelessness of mine but from a fine necessity—the bluefish had been feeding on small fish—sand eels—and its stomach, like a red and tensile purse, was stuffed full. Pieces of sand eels fell out, and among them maybe a half dozen were intact, squirming, unhurt in fact. So quickly, without a moment's warning, does the miraculous swerve and point to us, demanding that we be its willing servant. Swifter than thought my hands scooped them, and plunged them into the cold water, and the film of their siblings' death fell from them. For an instant they throbbed in place, too dazed to understand that they could swim back into life—and then they uncurled, like silver leaves, and flashed away.

Four Companions
with a Zest for Life

I've been teaching this year, something I don't do very
often, and so I've been pretty busy—*very* busy—and
my frequently heard complaint is for more time and
vitality than I can press out of the passing days. I like
to teach, but I don't like to give up anything else—
writing, walking, and of course the important "idling
and dreaming" that every poet must do. Lately I've
found myself reaching for the books of certain familiar
writers, whose own zest and energy offer some kindly
remedy to my condition.

Of course I live more than one life all the time
anyway. Don't we all, who read books? I am heading
off to a three-thirty class, carrying a folder of student
poems; but I walk across the campus as in a dress of
light—I am really in Alaska, strolling over one or two
glaciers with John Muir; or I am at the ocean, gazing
into the arc of the cresting wave with Henry Beston;
or I am in a sun-parched field with J. Henri Fabre,
looking with him at the cicada of the summer, "his
three stemmata, like little ruby telescopes...." Or
I am with Audubon, not in the green glades of

Louisiana, but in a chilly room in England, while he paints—"fourteen hours without fatigue." Think of that! Of dipping the brush, touching the canvas delicately, painting each single feather of some copper-feathered bird—hundreds of perfect, tiny, copper shields.

The writings of Audubon are curious. The public man is full of affectation; his adventures have all the mud and life stamped out of them. Alas! But the private man, who kept a journal for his wife while he lived in England, is relaxed, diligent, and eloquent. He is as charming by nature as the public man is charming by ambition.

And his daredevil ego—he would paint *every bird* in America—is matched by a boyish man's curiosity and energy. He is forever rising before dawn and tiptoeing out of some country house to take a walk. He buys two finches at a city fair and sets them free. He entertains an audience by painting with both hands at the same time. He gives money and clothes to a boy he meets, who clearly is on the last step to starvation. In York, walking along a stream in the evening, he sheds his clothes and takes "a dive smack across the creek." He walks miles in the early morning to visit an acquaintance and finds him "still snug asleep, so that I had enjoyed four and a half hours of life while he slept." And day after day he paints; his energy is prodigious.

In 1829, the year Audubon left England to return to America, J. Henri Fabre was six years old. He had already, by his own account, noticed many marvelous things on his grandparents' farm—he who was to become the noticer nonpareil. Don't be put off by his subject matter—the world of insects. Fabre is another Gulliver. He is unstinting in his patience and his enthusiasm as he searches the border between instinct and learned behavior, and his descriptions of the insect kingdom are close to miraculous. "There are fine ladies among them," he writes of the crab spiders, "who adorn their legs with a number of pink bracelets and their backs with carmine arabesques. . . ." Or, through his eyes, behold the praying mantis as she approaches her prey: "The murderous legs, originally folded and pressed together upon the chest, open wide, forming a cross with the body and revealing the arm-pits decorated with rows of beads and a black spot with a white dot in the centre."

Wonderfully too he describes himself on his way to study the hunting wasps: "A large umbrella saves me from sunstroke. It is the most scorching hour of the hottest day in the year. Exhausted by the heat, the Cicadae are silent. The bronze-eyed Gad-flies seek a refuge from the pitiless sun under the roof of my silken shelter. . . ." And on and on he goes, for eighty-eight years. What an example—what a long and happy life!

Henry Beston's story of living in the small house which he called the Fo'castle, on the last sweep of sand on Cape Cod, has been a favored book of many readers for a long time. Yet *The Outermost House* is forever new. First published in 1928 and still in print, it is as timeless as any book I know. Certainly if any book was written with one eye on the page and the other on the blue spread of the world beyond the window, this is it. Beston looks to the ritual *out there,* the year turning slowly and exquisitely and powerfully. No matter how many times one has read *The Outermost House,* with each reading Beston's attention and writing renew many facets of earthly and thalassic well-being.

He devotes a single chapter—and it is no brief chapter—to a description of his constant companion, the ocean wave, that form, that long tumult, that energy with its "wisps of watery noise, splashes and counter splashes, whispers, seethings, slaps, and chucklings." "Consider the marvel of what we see," he says. He describes waves which come onto the beach on quiet days, windy days, long days of storm, and nights too—for here is another earthling who would give up sleep, if he could, to remain every hour curious and in motion. "A storm surf . . . *grinds,* and this same long, sepulchral grinding—sound of utter terror to all mariners . . . is the cry of the breaker water roaring its way ashore and dragging at the sand."

Something about the "petal blue" of the summer ocean, a pool of color which Beston sometimes sees far out on quiet days, reminds me of the glaciers John Muir describes finding and exploring—Taku and Stickeen, or Muir Glacier itself in his book *Travels in Alaska.* "I greatly enjoyed my walk up this majestic ice-river," he writes, "charmed by the pale-blue, ineffably fine light in the crevasses, moulins, and wells, and the innumerable azure pools in basins of azure ice, and the network of surface streams, large and small, gliding, swirling with wonderful grace of motion in their frictionless channels. . . ." Amen. But this is only a single sentence. Are you ready for more? John Muir is ready—restless, unwilling to give over a single day to idleness; he is always on the move, climbing, looking, describing—a young man, a grown man, an old man with his alpenstock and his still-hungry heart.

On Muir Glacier his eyes inflame from the light. He can scarcely see. He makes a snow poultice; he fashions a pair of goggles; he kindles a fire in "a little can, a small campfire, the smallest I ever made or saw," and has a cup of tea. He soon describes himself as "refreshed," and is up and exploring the glacier's illuminated surface again. "After my twelve-mile walk, I ate a cracker and planned the camp," he says on another day. The northern lights flow over the sky: "Then losing all thought of sleep, I ran back to my cabin, carried out blankets and lay down on the moraine to keep watch until daybreak, that none of the sky wonders of the glorious night within reach of my eyes might be lost."

And I too am informed, dazzled, and refreshed— no longer too busy, no longer weary. Is there another glacier, an ocean, a sun-baked countryside, a dark stream, an eighteen-mile walk in my immediate future? Surely there is, and in such choice company, and I'm ready.

The Ponds

Great blue herons, like angels carved by Giacometti, are common. The edges of Clapp's Pond or Great Pond are good places to expect them. Occasionally they stay all winter, and I cannot imagine they have an easy time of it. We get little deep snow, for it melts usually in the salt-laden air between us and the mainland. But the ponds freeze, and the marshes. Green herons are also common; every year a pair nests somewhere along the edge of Little Sister Pond.

American egrets come, more often than not in late summer but sometimes earlier. They are a stark white in the intensely green salt marsh at the west end of town. Snowy egrets appear from time to time and prowl the edges of the larger ponds. They hunt with small, silky motions. Their long necks bend a little to the right, a little to the left, while their eyes stare with a mad concentration into the shallow water.

Occasionally a little blue heron, an adult bird, appears in the thick waters of summer, which stir fitfully under the spindles of its legs.

Very early one morning, in late summer, twelve

glossy ibis, flashing dark lights of purple and black, strolled the edges of Blackwater Pond.

The center of my landscape is a place called Beech Forest. On this sandy peninsula, the tall beeches with their cool, thick, lime-colored leaves are rare, and their deep, slow lives are recognized in this name-place. Most of these ponds have traditional names. Those without, I have named. Why not? The ponds are up-risings from the water table, shallow and shape-shifting as sand from the dunes blows into them, creating mass here, causing the water to spread in a generally southeast direction, away from the prevail-ing winter winds which day after day bite and rasp and shovel up the great weight of the sand.

There are pickerel in the ponds. Other fish too, I do not know their names. But I have seen them, on misty mornings, leaping from the pewter water. They are full of bones and I do not know anyone who eats them, though fishermen come in the spring and cast for them. They throw them back, or leave them, dead or alive, on the shores.

The cattails begin to rise in April; toward the end of that month of general upwelling, the stalks are thick and high enough for one to gather the pale green nutritious plaits. Golden club rises too, especially along the edges of Blackwater Pond. The wood ducks are fond of it, and the muskrats.

The frogs begin to sing any time from late March

to the second week in April, and they will be noisy and lusty until the end of the month, both in the ponds proper and in the even more shallow marshes and ephemeral pools.

In April, the snapping turtles wake from their long sleep. Sometimes they will float awhile, in a lonely exhaustion, on the surface of the pond, before a vigor fills their powerful bodies again. Once, on the narrow path between Great Pond and Little Sister Pond, my dog lingered, then came along slowly, mouthing something. He spit into my hand an enormous, curved claw. I knew immediately what it was. Some snapping turtles I have seen had heads like the heads of muskrats, and feet the size of a one-year-old child. One, a few years ago, emerged gargantuan and wrinkled among the pond lilies and slouched—its gassy breath coming and going softly, its pouchy throat expanding and contracting—across the muddy shallows. I didn't see it kill anything. Sometimes we get just enough, not too much. Did He who made the lily make you too? I said to it, looking into its unflickering eyes. You know it, the old shag-face answered, and slid back into the pond's black oils.

More young geese and ducks vanish from the water than live to flex their wings. I have found the bones of birds near the dens of foxes, but it is primarily the snapping turtles, watching from beneath the pond surface for the leaflike feet of the young birds to go paddling by, who contrive these disappearances.

Painted turtles are here too, and are common. Also

I have seen spotted turtles, in Blackwater Pond, or, at egg-laying time, trudging uphill from the water, or through the damp leaves around the pond.

An aerial view makes sense of the ponds—they are lined up and run from northeast to southwest. As wind and tide moved glacial debris from what is now the outer shore of Truro, and shoaled and packed it into the sweet curve which finishes this cape, an inner depression was formed, and therein lies one of the ponds. As the cape thickened, this depression re-adjusted, and another "eye" was created, and another pond. Let us send someone back in a few hundred thousand years to see what new ponds may have curled into birth. Unless, of course, the mechanisms have reversed, and there be nothing at all to report but the rising, unopposable sea.

Mallards are here, and black ducks. The mallards stay on the ponds, the black ducks spend time on the bay as well as on fresh water. Blue-winged teal migrate through, and green-winged. I have seen green-winged with young, but the dreamlike blue-winged, with the thin white moon on his face, I see only in the spring and the fall. I saw wood ducks here for the first time in 1977. There are now many nesting pairs.

Ring-necked ducks appear from time to time during migration, and then fly on. Red-breasted mergansers sometimes come over to the ponds from the salt water. In 1985, a shoveler spent a spring morning on

Blackwater Pond. Once, in late March 1991, a single hooded merganser appeared on Oak-Head Pond.

Winter ducks on the ponds include bufflehead, many of them, and goldeneyes, and coots, and pied-billed grebes. They all stay well into April.

In May, and you can trust your life to this, loons will fly over the woods and the ponds—the town, too—crying, in the early morning.

Both black-backed gulls and herring gulls come to the ponds and splash vigorously, to wash the salt away. Occasionally, in summer, least terns will fly over to Great Pond, and feed there.

The Canada geese—not the flocks that pass without a missed beat overhead, but the nesting pairs and the adolescents that stay throughout the year—are partly wild, partly tame. They are noisy in the air, secretive on the ponds while nesting is going on. Some years there are many young geese, other years there are few. Ask the turtles about it.

One spring I visited every day with a family of young geese, among which there was one whose wings did not develop. The rest of its body grew, the other feathers sprang from their sheaths and lengthened. But the wings remained small and unfeathered. It vanished, one night, to the oblivion of the ill-made, nature's dark throat, try again. The rest of them soon lost their shyness of me, and would climb over my body as I lay beside the pond or wait for me under the pine trees and leap out, a cloud of gray laughers, when I appeared.

By August, the young geese are strong fliers, and the parents take them from the ponds down to the marshes and the shore, where some of them will spend the winter near the salt water. Others fly off, looking for new homelands.

In spring the water of the pond is like blue wool, endlessly tossing. The heavy, cold water has sunk to the black bottom of the pond and, struck by this weight, the bottom water stirs and rises, filling the pond's basins with wild nutrition. It is an annual event, necessary to the appetite of the year. In late spring, the green grasses and reeds break through, and the first foils of the lilies. The wind grows calmer.

I sit at the edge of Great Pond. The morning light strikes the mist and begins to dispel it. On the pond two geese are floating. Beneath them their reflected images glide; between them five goslings are paddling. The goslings have only recently emerged from the grassy hummock of birth and already they are slipping along eagerly on this glassy road. As instantly as they know hunger, they begin to reach out for duckweed, insects, the tips of grasses.

Occasionally I lean forward and gaze into the water. The water of a pond is a mirror of roughness and honesty—it gives back not only my own gaze, but the nimbus of the world trailing into the picture on all sides. The swallows, singing a little as they fly back and forth across the pond, are flying therefore over my shoulders, and through my hair. A turtle passes slowly across the muddy bottom, touching my cheekbone. If at this moment I heard a clock ticking, would I remember what it was, what it signified?

It is summer now, the geese have grown, the reeds are a bearded green flocculence, full of splinters of light. Across the pond, the purple loosestrife (alien here but what does that mean—it is recklessly gorgeous) has come into bloom. A fox steps from the woods, its shoulders are bright, its narrow chest is as white as milk. The wild eyes stare at the geese. Daintily it walks to the pond's edge, calmly it drinks. Then the quick head lifts and turns, with a snap, and once again the geese are appraised. Perhaps it looks toward me too. But I am utterly quiet, and half-hidden. The wind is on my side—I am a stone with its feet in the mud. While I watch, the fox lies down beside the purple flowers. For a while it watches the geese, then the lithe body shrugs to a position of comfort among the leaves and the blossoms, and it sleeps.

Pen and Paper
and a Breath of Air

For at least thirty years, and at almost all times, I have carried a notebook with me, in my back pocket. It has always been the same kind of notebook—small, three inches by five inches, and hand-sewn. By no means do I write poems in these notebooks. And yet over the years the notebooks have been laced with phrases that eventually appear in poems. So, they are the pages upon which I begin. Also I record various facts which are permanently or temporarily important to me—when I first see certain birds in the spring, addresses, quotes from books I'm reading, things people say, shopping lists, recipes, thoughts.

Some of the phrases and ideas written down in the notebooks never make the leap into finished prose or poems. They do not elaborate themselves in my unconscious thoughts, apparently, nor does my conscious mind pluck at them. This does not necessarily mean that they are of a casual or fleeting order of things; it could be that they are seeds broadcast on a chilly day—their time has not yet come. Often I find the same idea will emerge through several phrases before it gets worked on.

I don't use the pages front to back, but randomly, in a disorderly way. I write wherever I happen to open the notebook. I don't know why this is. When the notebook is fairly full, I start another. In the spring and fall notebooks especially, there are pages where the writing is blurred and hard to read. Spring and fall are the rainy seasons, and almost all of the entries are made somewhere out-of-doors.

What I write down is extremely exact in terms of phrasing and of cadence. In an old notebook I can find, "look the trees / are turning / their own bodies / into pillars of light." In a more recent notebook, "the refined anguish of language / passed over him." Sometimes what is written down is not generally understandable at all, but is a kind of private shorthand. The entry "6/8/92 woof!" records for me that on this day, and with this very doggy sound, I first came upon coyotes in the Provincelands. Both the shorthand and the written phrase are intended to return me to the moment and place of the entry. I mean this very exactly. The words do not take me to the reason I made the entry, but back to the felt experience, whatever it was. This is important. I can, then, think forward again to the idea—that is, the significance of the event—rather than back upon it. It is the instant I try to catch in the notebooks, not the comment, not the thought. And, of course, this is so often what I am aiming to do in the finished poems themselves.

Excerpts

Who would tell the mockingbird his song is frivolous,
since it lacks words?

———

Do you think the wren ever dreams of a better house?

———

Though you have not seen them, there are swans, even
    now
tapping from the egg and emerging
   into the sunlight.
They know who they are.

———

When will you have a little pity for
every soft thing
that walks through the world,
yourself included?

———

When the main characters of one's life die, is there any
replacement? Or, is there anything *but* replacement?

———

I hope I don't live to be a hundred
in the arms of my family.

———

When you first saw her—beauty, the dream—the human vortex of your life—or him—did you stop, and stand in the crisp air, breathing like a tree? Did you change your life?

———————

The small deadly voice
of vanity.

———————

It's better for the heart to break
than not to break.

———————

Elly Ameling during a masterclass at Tanglewood, talking to a young singer: "No! No! No! Make it like peaches in your mouth!"

———————

All my life, and it has not come to any more than this: beauty and terror.

———————

Something totally unexpected,
like a barking cat.

———————

Sharpsburg: "One well-read member of the 9th New York wrote long afterward: The mental strain was so great that I saw at that moment the singular effect mentioned, I think, in the life of Goethe on a similar occasion—the whole landscape for an instant turned slightly red."

—B. Catton, *Mr. Lincoln's Army*

————

The sword, after all, is not built just to glitter like a ribbon in the air.

————

But I want to say something more uncomfortable even than that.

————

"And then, who knows? Perhaps we will be taken in hand by certain memories, as if by angels."

—M. Yourcenar

————

Molasses, an orange, fennel seed, anise seed, rye flour, two cakes of yeast.

————

Culture: power, money, and security (therefore).
Art: hope, vision, the soul's need to speak.

————

All culture developed as some wild, raw creature strived to live better and longer.

————

Dreams don't have time/space constriction. Of course, in a way Adam naming the things of this world was narrowing his horizons.

Perhaps dreaming is meditating, before language existed. Animals certainly dream.

———

Language, the tool of consciousness.

———

The line is the device upon which the poem spins itself into being. Verse, versus, *vers,* turn the plough, turn the line. It is impossible to measure the frustration I feel when, after making careful decisions about where the lines should turn, an editor snaps off the long limbs to fit some magazine's column-girth or print-line.

———

Who are you? They called out, at the edge of the village.
I am one of you, the poet called back.
Though he was dressed like the wind, though he looked like
a waterfall.

———

F. has been to visit us, and now he is gone. The power of last resort, is the power to disrupt.

———

M. arranging the curtains in the next room. "Hello there, darling moon," I hear her say.

———

If you kill for knowledge, what is the name of what you have lost?

———

The danger of people becoming infatuated with knowledge. Thoreau gassing the moth to get a perfect specimen. Audubon pushing the needle into the bittern's heart.

———

I took the fox bones back into the dunes and buried them. I don't want to hold on to such things anymore. I mean, I'm certainly full of admiration, and curiosity. But I think something else—a reverence that disavows keeping things—must come to us all, sooner or later. Like a gift, an understanding, a more happy excitement than possession. Or, of a sudden—too late!— like a stone between the eyes.

———

Everybody has to have their little tooth of power. Everybody wants to be able to bite.

———

About poems that don't work—who wants to see a bird almost fly?

With what sugar in your voice would you persuade
the beach plum
to hurry?

After a cruel childhood, one must reinvent oneself.
Then reimagine the world.

---

van Gogh—he considered everything, and still went
crazy with rapture.

A snapping turtle was floating today on Little Sister
    Pond.
Goldeneyes still on Great Pond.

Laughing gulls fly by the house laughing.
Maybe a hundred pilot whales off the point.

All July and into August, Luke and I see foxes. An
adult fox with a young pup. The adult serious and
nervous and quick. The young one trailing behind,
not serious. It reached up, swatted the pine boughs
with a black paw before it vanished under the trees.

To Unity College, in Maine, and back. We stayed in Waterville, saw two bald eagles flying over open rivers, though there was still much ice, and snow. A good trip, friendly people, an interested audience. Luke and Bear were quiet throughout, except that Bear threw up on me just as we arrived in the parking lot. I hope he learns to ride better than that.

———

Hundreds of gannets feeding just offshore, plunging, tufts of water rising with a white up-kick. Scary birds, long wings, very white, fearful-looking beaks. We opened the car windows and there was no sound but the sound of their wings rustling. They fed at three or four places, then were gone much farther out. We were at the right place at the right time.

———

"I am doing pretty well, gathering energy, working . . . and every now and then *timor mortis* descends over me like midnight."

Letter from D. H.

———

Just at the lacy edge of the sea, a dolphin's skull. Recent, but perfectly clean. And entirely beautiful. I held it in my hands, I was so excited I was breathless. What will I do?

———

Three deer near the path to Oak Head—of course
now they always make me think of Luke. Happiness
by association.

————

Who knows, maybe the root is the flower
of that other life.

————

Money, in our culture, is equal to power. And money,
finally, means very little because power, in the end,
means nothing.

————

Lee, as he was dying, called out, "Strike the tent!"
Stonewall Jackson said at the end, softly as I imagine
it, "Let us cross over the river and rest under the shade
of the trees."

————

Today I am altogether without ambition. Where did I
get such wisdom?

————

You there, like a red fist under my ribs—
be reasonable.

————

little myrtle warblers
kissing the air

Let's not pretend we know how the mule feels.

Hearing a crow, the first one in a long time. I listened to it, deeply and with pleasure. And I thought: what if I were dead, lying there dead, and *I heard that!*

Which would you rather be, intellectually deft, or spiritually graceful?

The sugar of vanity, the honey of truth.

When I was young, I was attracted to sorrow. It seemed interesting. It seemed an energy that would take me somewhere. Now I am older, if not old, and I hate sorrow. I see that it has no energy of its own, but uses mine, furtively. I see that it is leaden, without breath, and repetitious, and unsolvable.

And now I see that I am sorrowful about only a few things, but over and over.

Fairy tales—the great difference is between doing

something, and doing nothing. Always, in such tales, the hero or heroine does *something*.

————————

The new baby is all awash with glory.
She has a cry that says *I'm here! I'm here!*

————————

Give me that dark moment I will carry it everywhere like a mouthful of rain.

————————

There is a place
in the woods
where my swift
and stout-hearted dog
turns and wants to climb

into my arms.

————————

Don't engage in too much fancy footwork before you strike a blow.

————————

So much of what Woolf wrote she wrote not because she was a woman, but because she was Woolf.

————————

I would like to do whatever it is that presses the essence from the hour.

A fact: one picks it up and reads it, and puts it down, and there is an end to it. But an idea! That one may pick up, and reflect upon, and oppose, and expand, and so pass a delightful afternoon altogether.

From my way of thinking, Thoreau frequently seems an overly social person.

The cry of the killdeer / like a tiny sickle.

The translation of experience into contemplation, and the placement of this contemplation within the formality of a certain kind of language, with no intent to make contact—be it across whatever thin or wild a thread—with the spiritual condition of the reader, is not poetry. Archibald MacLeish: Here is the writer, and over there—there is "the mystery of the universe." The poem exists—indeed, gets itself written—in the relation *between* the man and the world. The three ingredients of poetry: the mystery of the universe, spiritual curiosity, the energy of language.

And what is the universe, as far as we are concerned?

Leo Frobenius: "It was first the animal world, in its various species, that impressed mankind as a mystery, and that, in its character of admired immediate neighbor, evoked the impulse to imitative identification. Next, it was the vegetable world and the miracle of the fruitful earth, wherein death is changed into life. And finally . . . the focus of attention lifted to the mathematics" of the heavens.

Art cannot separate from these first examples which willed it into existence. Say such forces belong now only to dream or nightmare or to Jung's (our) collective unconscious—or to the ecologically sensitive— I say it's entirely more primal than that. Poetry was born in the relationship between men of earth and the earth itself. Without perceptual experience of life on this earth, how could the following lines be meaningful?

It is the east, and Juliet is the sun. Or,

And what rough beast, its hour come round at last,
Slouches toward Bethlehem to be born?

I think as an ecologist. But I feel as a member of a great family—one that includes the elephant and the wheat stalk as well as the schoolteacher and the industrialist. This is not a mental condition, but a spiritual condition. Poetry is a product of our history, and our history is inseparable from the natural world. Now, of course, in the hives and dungeons of the cities, poetry cannot console, it carries no weight, for the pact between the natural world and the individual has been broken. There is no more working for harvest—only hunting, for profit. Lives are no longer exercises in pleasure and valor, but only the means to the amassment of worldly goods. If poetry is ever to become meaningful to such persons, *they* must take the first step—away from their materially bound and self-interested lives, toward the trees, and the waterfall. It is not poetry's fault that it has so small an audience, so little effect upon the frightened, money-loving world. Poetry, after all, is not a miracle. It is an effort to formalize (ritualize) individual moments and the transcending effects of these moments into a music that all can use. It is the song of our species.

———

Hasn't the end of the world been coming absolutely forever?

———

It takes about
seventy hours to drag
a poem into
the light.

———

delirious with certainty

It's almost six A.M. The mockingbird is still singing. I'm on my way to the ocean, with the sun, just rising, on my left shoulder, and the moon, like a circle of pale snow, lingering on my right.

Fry

Thousands of small fish are moving along in the shallows: a flock, a flight under the weight of the water, dipping and rising, loose-spined; their fins, rowing, are minute and precise; they are energy-packets; six would fit into a thimble, all gauze and glaze, and all translucent—the pipeline of appetite clear in each body. Thousands and thousands—a throng of rainbows, a pod, an enormous pack, yet they swing along as a single rainbow, one wing, one thing, one traveler. Their mouths are open, fierce colanders scooping in the diatoms. They turn to the right, the left. They dash and hover. . . .

It is summer, the long twilight. I stare and stare into the water. I say to myself, *which one am I?*

Staying Alive

We are walking along the path, my dog and I, in the blue half-light. My dog, no longer young, steps carefully on the icy path, until he catches the scent of the fox. This morning the fox runs out onto the frozen pond, and my dog follows. I stand and watch them. The ice prevents either animal from getting a good toe-grip, so they move with the big-hearted and curvaceous motions of running, but in slow motion. All the way across they stay the same distance apart—the fox can go no faster, neither can my long-legged old dog, who will ache from this for a week. The scene is original and pretty as a dream. But I am wide awake. Then the fox vanishes among the yellow weeds on the far side of the pond, and my dog comes back, panting.

I believe everything has a soul.

Adults can change their circumstances; children cannot. Children are powerless, and in difficult situations they are the victims of every sorrow and mischance and rage around them, for children feel all of these things but without any of the ability that adults have to change them. Whatever can take a child beyond such circumstances, therefore, is an alleviation and a blessing.

I quickly found for myself two such blessings—the natural world, and the world of writing: literature. These were the gates through which I vanished from a difficult place.

In the first of these—the natural world—I felt at ease; nature was full of beauty and interest and mystery, also good and bad luck, but never misuse. The second world—the world of literature—offered me, besides the pleasures of form, the sustentation of empathy (the first step of what Keats called negative capability) and I ran for it. I relaxed in it. I stood willingly and gladly in the characters of everything—other people, trees, clouds. And this is what I learned, that the world's *otherness* is antidote to confusion—that standing *within* this otherness—the beauty and the mystery of the world, out in the fields or deep inside books—can re-dignify the worst-stung heart.

———

The thin red foxes would come together in the last weeks of winter. Then, their tracks in the snow were not of one animal but of two, where in the night they had gone running together. Neither were they the tracks of hunting animals, which run a straight if tacking line. These would sweep and glide, and stop to tussle. Behold a kicking up of snow, a heeling down, a spraying up of the sand beneath. Sometimes also I would hear them, in the distance—a yapping, a summons to hard and cold delight.

———

I learned to build bookshelves and brought books to my room, gathering them around me thickly. I read by day and into the night. I thought about perfectibility, and deism, and adjectives, and clouds, and the foxes. I locked my door, from the inside, and leaped from the roof and went to the woods, by day or darkness.

———

When the young are born, the dog fox hunts and leaves what he has caught at the den entrance. In the darkness below, under snags and roots of trees, or clumps of wild roses whose roots are as thick and long as ship ropes, the vixen stays with the young foxes. They press against her body and nurse. They are safe.

Once I put my face against the body of our cat as she lay with her kittens, and she did not seem to mind. So I pursed my lips against that full moon, and I tasted the rich river of her body.

———

I read my books with diligence, and mounting skill, and gathering certainty. I read the way a person might swim, to save his or her life. I wrote that way too.

———

After a few weeks the young foxes play about the den.
They are dark and woolly. They chew bones and
sticks, and each other. They growl. They play with
feathers. They fight over food, and the strongest eats
more and more often than the weakest. They have
neither mercy nor pity. They have one responsibility—
to stay alive, if they can, and be foxes. They grow
powerful, and thin, more and more toothy, and more
and more alert.

———

A summer day—I was twelve or thirteen—at my
cousins' house, in the country. They had a fox, collared
and on a chain, in a little yard beside the house. All
afternoon all afternoon all afternoon it kept—

*Once I saw a fox, in an acre of cranberries, leaping and
pouncing, leaping and pouncing, leaping and falling back,
its forelegs merrily slapping the air as it tried to tap a
yellow butterfly with its thin black forefeet, the butterfly
fluttering just out of reach all across the deep green gloss
and plush of the sweet-smelling bog.*

—it kept running back and forth, trembling and
chattering.

———

Once my father took me ice-skating, then forgot me, and went home. He was of course reminded that I had been with him, and sent back, but this was hours later. I had been found wandering over the ice and taken to the home of a kind, young woman, who knew my family slightly; she had phoned them to say where I was.

When my father came through the door, I thought—never had I seen so handsome a man; he talked, he laughed, his movements were smooth and easy, his blue eyes were clear. He had simply, he said, forgotten that I existed. One could see—I can see even now, in memory—what an alleviation, what a lifting from burden he had felt in those few hours. It lay on him, that freedom, like an aura. Then I put on my coat, and we got into the car, and he sat back in the awful prison of himself, the old veils covered his eyes, and he did not say another word.

I did not think of language as the means to self-description. I thought of it as the door—a thousand opening doors!—past myself. I thought of it as the means to notice, to contemplate, to praise, and, *thus,* to come into power.

In books: truth, and daring, passion of all sorts. Clear and sweet and savory emotion did not run in a rippling stream in my personal world—more pity to it! But in stories and poems I found passion unfettered, and healthy. Not that such feelings were always or even commonly found in their clearest, most delectable states in all the books I read. Not at all! I saw what skill was needed, and persistence—how one must bend one's spine, like a hoop, over the page—the long labor. I saw the difference between doing nothing, or doing a little, and the redemptive act of true effort. Reading, then writing, then desiring to write well, shaped in me that most joyful of circumstances—a passion for work.

———

Deep in the woods, I tried walking on all fours. I did it for an hour or so, through thickets, across a field, down to a cranberry bog. I don't think anyone saw me! At the end, I was exhausted and sore, but I had seen the world from the level of the grasses, the first bursting growth of trees, declivities, lumps, slopes, rivulets, gashes, open spaces. I was some slow old fox, wandering, breathing, hitching along, lying down finally at the edge of the bog, under the swirling rickrack of the trees.

———

You must not ever stop being whimsical.

———

And you must not, ever, give anyone else the responsibility for your life.

———

I don't mean it's easy or assured, there are the stubborn stumps of shame, grief that remains unsolvable after all the years, a bag of stones that goes with one wherever one goes and however the hour may call for dancing and for light feet. But there is, also, the summoning world, the admirable energies of the world, better than anger, better than bitterness and, because more interesting, more alleviating. And there is the thing that one does, the needle one plies, the work, and within that work a chance to take thoughts that are hot and formless and to place them slowly and with meticulous effort into some shapely heat-retaining form, even as the gods, or nature, or the soundless wheels of time have made forms all across the soft, curved universe—that is to say, having chosen to claim my life, I have made for myself, out of work and love, a handsome life.

Form is certainty. All nature knows this, and we have no greater adviser. Clouds have forms, porous and shape-shifting, bumptious, fleecy. They are what clouds need to be, to be clouds. See a flock of them come, on the sled of the wind, all kneeling above the blue sea. And in the blue water, see the dolphin built to leap, the sea mouse skittering, see the ropy kelp with its air-filled bladders tugging it upward; see the albatross floating day after day on its three-jointed wings. Each form sets a tone, enables a destiny, strikes a note in the

universe unlike any other. How can we ever stop looking? How can we ever turn away?

––––––––––

So, it comes first: the world. Then, literature. And then,
what one pencil moving over a thousand miles of paper
can (perhaps, sometimes) do.

––––––––––

The fox beside the icy pond had been feeding on an
old frozen raccoon, a bad heap, bones and tallow and
skin, but better than nothing. For weeks, on my early
walk along this path, I saw the fox as he dipped into
the dark dish of the frozen body, rasping and tearing.

––––––––––

And now my old dog is dead, and another I had after
him, and my parents are dead, and that first world,
that old house, is sold and lost, and the books I gathered there lost, or sold—but more books bought, and
in another place, board by board and stone by stone,
like a house, a true life built, and all because I was
steadfast about one or two things: loving foxes, and
poems, the blank piece of paper, and my own energy—and mostly the shimmering shoulders of the
world that shrug carelessly over the fate of any individual that they may, the better, keep the Niles and
the Amazons flowing.

   And that I did not give to anyone the responsibility for my life. It is mine. I made it. And can do what

I want to with it. Live it. Give it back, someday, without bitterness, to the wild and weedy dunes.

The fox is sitting on a sandy rise, it is looking at me. It yawns, the pickets of its teeth glitter. It scratches under its jaw, rises, and in slow, haunchy nonchalance leaps over the slopes of sand, then down a path, walking, then trotting; then it sprints into the shadows under the trees, as if into water, and is gone.

Steepletop

The phone rang. It was Edna Millay. She was crying, near hysteria. He thought she had been drinking. She said she was trying to find George Dillon.

Biographers, of all writers, have need of prayers, and answered prayers. The graceful angles and sinuations of clean prose may finally be chiseled from the language, but what about the material itself? How can the biographer know when enough is known, and known with sufficient certainty? What about secrets, what about errors, what about the small black holes where there is nothing at all? What about the wranglings among minor characters, the withholding of facts for thoughtful and not-so-thoughtful reasons—or their mishandling—and this not even in the present but in the past, hidden in letters, in remembered conversations, in reams of papers? And what about the waywardness of life itself—the proclivity toward randomness—the sudden meaningless uplift of wind that tosses out one sheet of paper and keeps another? What about the moment that speaks worlds, as the saying goes, but in the middle of the night, and into deaf ears, and so is never heard, or heard of?

I would not be a biographer for all the tea in China.

1.

In 1925, the poet Edna St. Vincent Millay and her husband Eugen Boissevain bought a farmhouse and some eight hundred acres of land surrounding it in upstate New York, near the town of Austerlitz. It would be their home for the next twenty-five years. They named the house Steepletop, after a wildflower common in the area, a field flower primarily, with a pale pink, or sometimes a deep pink, slightly tilting crest of small blossoms.

When they died—Boissevain in the late summer of 1949 and Millay a little over a year later—the poet's sister Norma Millay Ellis and her husband Charles Ellis went to live there. I was then fifteen, a schoolgirl in Ohio, reading poetry and wanting to write poetry. I wrote a letter to Norma Millay asking if I could visit Steepletop, and she replied that I could. In June of 1953—the morning after I graduated from the local high school—I left Ohio. It took me two days to drive across Ohio, through Pennsylvania, and on to Austerlitz, New York, then find the twisty dirt road out of the village and up into the hills, to the poet's house.

I stayed three days. I returned again at the end of the summer, then the next winter, and then, in a more or less permanent manner, I moved in.

There are safe, hazy, public names for what I became: secretary, amanuensis, companion. They don't, of course, give the substance of it. I was company to a difficult, egocentric woman who was saddled as well as favored by the tasks and the power which became hers as executor of her sister's literary estate. Over the months, I became useful, also companionable, agreeable, and loyal. I was young, and deeply moved by the intimacy of living in the poet's house, among her possessions. If Norma was eccentric, she was also intelligent, racy, tender, persuasive, and dramatic. Certainly I had known no one like her in Ohio.

By attitude, by kindnesses, I was made to feel a part of the family, and Charlie and Norma talked openly to me about the poet's life. Some of the stories I have forgotten surely, others were *stapled* to my mind. Some of the stories went so far back as the Millay girls' childhood in Maine, others were about professional matters, the years in New York, still others about life at Steepletop. Many of them were simply the anecdotal incidentals one is apt to keep remembering about someone who is gone, and is missed.

There were, also, the less happy stories, involving illness, sex, weaknesses of various kinds, and, importantly, other people. Norma called them "secrets," and she meant by that word, I believe, to convey a sense of intimacy with me (she was "giving" me these secrets) and, additionally, to control the information even after it was given (I was to hold on to these secrets but I was not to do anything with them). Each of these stories I

was told in the deepest confidence; each of these stories, I was made to understand, could hurt the repu-
tation of the poet if known to the public, or hurt
persons still living, or—and in some cases this seemed
reasonable—the stories were too private, or inexplica-
ble, or grievous, or silly, to be talked about. What was
I, then, expected to do with these "secrets"? I don't
know. I know only that it was an obvious relief to
Norma to shed them, and that, puzzling, delicious, or
burdensome though they sometimes were, they were
my portion. My job, primarily, was to listen and to
remember.

To attend to the work of organizing her sister's papers,
Norma Millay had set up an office in the dining
room.* So, in that gracious room, filing cabinets stood
next to the corner cupboards, which were filled with
the flutings and the lace and the tiny spars of shells
the poet had collected on the beaches of Florida and
elsewhere. Norma Millay did not steer with the wheel
of neatness; the room was cluttered with piles of
materials dealt with or to be dealt with soon—or
eventually.

Under the papers and books, under the boxes,

---

*Millay herself had no office as such; she wrote in her bedroom, or the
library, or the small cabin built for her by Mr. Robert Herron of Austerlitz; it stood in a tangle of young white pines, some distance from the
house.

against the wall, stood an old-fashioned flat-topped trunk. In this trunk, Norma said one day, were the letters George Dillon had written to Edna Millay. Certainly, by this time, I had learned the language of innuendo and suggestion—it was a large trunk. After that I began to hear, story by story, somewhat of the depth and the breadth of passion, risk, disquietude, sacrifice, and whatever else goes into the tearing up of hearts. The relationship between Edna St. Vincent Millay and George Dillon was one of the heavy, if not one of the leaden, secrets. Remember, you mustn't tell! Norma would say, striking in a single phrase both of her usual admonitions. George Dillon, in the time I am speaking of, was still alive. It had been an "extramarital" affair, to give it its dullest name, in what was certainly a more private if not a more innocent time. Poets in those years did not rush to confession, readers did not hurry to conclusion. I was told about other affairs that Millay had, how they burned, or smoldered, and were finished. The affair with George Dillon was something else, it did not die out. For years the three of them, Millay, Dillon, and Boissevain, made accommodation to it.

Other thoughts occur to me. By so fiercely calling this affair (and other matters also) a secret, wasn't Norma, whose tendency toward the dramatic was sometimes shrill, sometimes drowsy, but never entirely stilled, prodding and even ramping my attention? Of course she was. In fact, there wasn't a great deal of interest in the poet in those years—the poet's life was to a certain extent our household drama. Also, Norma talked continually about her intention to write the poet's biography. She might have worried, I suppose, that I would run off with the goods.

But, no. I think Norma found in me something needful or at least easeful to her at that time. I think she doubted her ability to write a biography, and she was in the uncomfortable position of being unable to select, from all that was not written down, what was important from what was not important—or, more severely, what was proper biographical material from what was not. And I was there—an audience of one. So, over the years, stories sad and mirthful, important or slight, were dropped into my ears. I questioned nothing, not wanting to break what often seemed like a spell. I simply stopped whatever I was doing, and heard the stories. They could have been mathematical equations. They could have been songs.

2.

Edna St. Vincent Millay, in the twenties, must have been an astonishment. With her flaming red hair, her dramatic dress, her poems spinning with their light feet across conventional behavior, she must have moved like a fire over the hearts of her audience— souls that had never yet broken the rules must have ached toward transgression, believing, under the influence, that to do so was to discover otherwise undiscoverable raptures. Millay was, in those years, one of the banner carriers of women's freedom, and intellect, and creative force. For one young man in particular, she must have seemed as powerful and amazing as anything his nimble brain had ever met.

In the best tradition—the Godwinian, or, more accurately, the Shelleyan—Millay did indeed ascribe to the rights of passion, the equality of the sexes, and to the freedom of marriage partners; and she did have love affairs, and not behind doors or in scamping hideaways but with her husband's acknowledgment. All of which, as I say, was nothing new—not the idea of it. But who knows, ever, about any individual—a thirty-five-year-old poet with wild red hair included—whether subscription is to the idea alone, or its enactment.

I do not think that in Chicago, in 1927, a good-looking young poet and university student named George Dillon, meeting Edna St. Vincent Millay for the first time, could have imagined, in his wildest, most lawless dreams, that their tangled future was as possible as it was. Do you see what I mean? That there was an instant attraction between the two is easy to imagine, and has been recorded by one person at least who was witness to it. That the moment would be sustained for years, leading Dillon irretrievably into rapture, poetry, and a final infrangible silence, was something no one could have guessed—fate steps, like the most casual if gorgeously dressed sword carrier, onto the stage.

They met at the University of Chicago, where George Dillon was still a student. Dillon, on behalf of the reading series, had invited Millay to come and read her poems, on a November evening. Among the

unpublished papers of Gladys Campbell, a graduate
student at the University and a friend of Dillon's, there
is a description of this evening.* Millay and Dillon,
also Campbell, met backstage. Eugen Boissevain was
there. Millay, as usual for her, was nervous; Boissevain
was reassuring and charming. Gladys Campbell re-
members the moment when Millay, on the stage, out
of the silence a reader gathers and lets hover before
starting, began to read her poems in that way she had,
commanding and flirtatious at once, and with an ac-
cent developed more from a geography of the mind
than any part of the world. Campbell recalls how Dillon reached over and gripped her wrist, in the wildest
way. Later, at the home of a friend, Millay and Dillon
talked together, and Dillon recited some of his poems.
After this meeting, the two of them began to corre-
spond. The following summer, Dillon went to Steepletop for the first time.

Gladys Campbell and others who knew young
George Dillon recall his mature mind, his personal
reserve, and his stunning physical beauty. He was tall
and lean, a good swimmer and a long-distance runner,
a young man with impeccable manners. He was already serving his second year as an associate editor of
Poetry, at the invitation of Harriet Monroe. And Viking had just published his first book of poems, *Boy in
the Wind,* a youthful and lyrical collection of poems

---

*University of Virginia Library, Charlottesville, Special Collections.

which tended, in their formal stanzas, to display smoke rather than fire. But it was elegant smoke. His attitude to poetry, one might say, was respectful, but the poems themselves were a little empty. Perhaps his uncommon reserve curbed the tendency toward innovation, and energetic broil, that one thinks of in connection with youthful writing. The book is musical, a little vapid. Dillon seemed, in this book, a talent waiting for a subject.

There are many hints and also explicit telling references, in letters, in poems, in addresses, should one want them, should one feel compelled to read into them, or out of them, the heat, and the flavor, the star-shape, the rapture, the separations, the dailiness, the cruelty, the slyness, the fun, the intensity of the affair between Edna St. Vincent Millay and George Dillon. It went on for years—Dillon coming to live at Steeple-top; Dillon and Millay in New York; the two of them in Paris, where Dillon later had an apartment near the Square Lamartine; or at Steepletop while Eugen went to Ragged Island, in Maine. The sequence of sonnets by Millay called *Fatal Interview* was written of it, as was George Dillon's second and last book of poems, *The Flowering Stone*. Both books were published in 1931.*

---

*Even so powerfully as I know this to be so, as I write the line I feel the presumption of saying *it is so*. Let me revise therefore: "Both books, *Fatal*

In the world at large, not privately or in the poems, they lived their passion discreetly. It was a different world then; the public appetite for private material had not yet formed, or been formed. But, on the other hand, they did not belie the truth. In Elizabeth Atkins's book *Edna St. Vincent Millay and Her Times,** Eugen Boissevain is quoted as giving to Ms. Atkins— "in a deeply bitten marginal comment on my manuscript"—the information, explicitly stated, that the poems of *Fatal Interview* took their genesis from an affair which his wife had had with another man during their marriage.

They lived at times in Paris. George Dillon began to translate poems from Baudelaire's *Les Fleurs du Mal.* Then Millay began to do so also, and soon the number of poems translated was substantial; Harpers published the book, co-authored, in 1936. And then, the brave human heart, in spite of all its promises and intentions, spoke out.

Said Norma: After years of it, Eugen finally went

Interview and *The Flowering Stone,* were written just beyond the first years of their affair.

There are letters (Millay to Dillon) in which it is written down that the sonnets of *Fatal Interview* are to or about Dillon. So I'm not talking about doubt, but about something else. I mean, a necessary modesty—an acknowledgment of the impregnable complexity of the event itself, a mist that surrounds it forever—a dignity nothing can ever completely trespass.

*(Chicago: The University of Chicago Press, 1936), p. 200.

alone to the island, leaving them at Steepletop. Then he said to Vincent, you have to choose. So she did.

George Dillon is almost unknown to this generation. His second book of poems, *The Flowering Stone*, received the Pulitzer Prize in 1933—Dillon was then twenty-five years old, the youngest poet ever to be so honored. The lyrical voice of his earlier poems is here thickened and deepened, but the mood is dark throughout. Human love, passionate and irresistible, is deflected from any sense of festival, celebration, even longevity, by intimations of abandonment. Indeed the tone of his work reveals none of the fervor and self-confidence one would wish a young writer to have—that bulk and fire against which the pain and the complexities of life could rub, without erasing the developing man. What the poems have, so early, is a sense of conclusion—of life in retreat. They speak of a sensibility utterly shaken—as young trees, the most slender and limber, are shaken by storm, and yet survive, though barely.

> *Indeed, when it is done, incredible youth told over,*
> *The time sweet and shameful, the issues shocking and*
> *   sweet,*
> *And his life lying calm on a litter of leaves at his feet,*
> *A man would be nothing but that he has been a lover,*
> *He is glad for that. . . .* *

---

*From *The Flowering Stone* (New York: Viking Press, 1931), p. 30.

If a man wishes to be private, all but invisible, who shall dissuade him? George Dillon continued to serve as editor of *Poetry* and to translate from the work of Ronsard and Racine. But he wrote no more poems. In a letter to a friend he said—I paraphrase slightly—that he had studied as to the cause of his inability to write, and thought he understood it, yet understanding was far from a cure.*

Finally he retired from *Poetry* and moved to Charleston, South Carolina. Friends say he remained kind, quiet, well-mannered. They say his good looks did not leave him. They say he was, always, ferociously private. And that he had, always, three photographs above his desk: one of his mother, one of a friend from the early years in Chicago, and one of Edna Millay.

3.

In 1963, I went to England. I had already left Steepletop and was returning there only occasionally. I had met someone, fallen in love. As a result I had discovered that I was attached to Steepletop by a possessiveness that was adhesive, and would brook no such independence. So I went away.

Norma, I heard, was still planning to write a book about her sister, but she did not. Once, in the seventies, I went back to visit but, of course, nothing was the

---

*University of Virginia Library, Special Collections.

same. I was no longer a child; I wanted no more secrets; the old bonds would not adjust.

Over the years I did not talk often about my own
life at Steepletop, and seldom, indeed, about Millay, or
Millay and Dillon. In the way that I learned what I
learned, privacy and loyalty went deeply hand in
hand. Millay was a felt presence at Steepletop, a spirit,
the heart of the house and our lives. How often I felt,
standing in one room or another, that she had just
gone—that I had just missed her, by a split second
perhaps. Which is to say, altogether. Perhaps I keep
what I have learned about her for the very personal
purpose of assuagement—of *knowing* her, of recogniz-
ing some of her private virtues and follies in a way
that is intimate, protective, untradable. My relationship with Norma did nothing to lessen this hold on
me, and, in fact, she had ways to bind me more closely
into this house and its spirit. "She would have liked
you," she might say. "You are our little sister," she
might say. These were not kindnesses, not altogether.

And this too should be said. I believed then, and
believe still, the stories I heard—funny, complex,
sometimes courageous, sometimes frightening—about
Millay. They were, however, Norma's stories. The two
sisters without any doubt had a relationship that included, among other things, intimacy, aggression, and
unusual confidence. I do not think that Norma Millay
ever lied to me, at least I think she never meant to. But
to hold anyone responsible for truth, that cold goddess,
is foolish; Norma told me what Norma knew, which

is partly what her sister told her, partly what she observed, and partly what she interpreted from the point of being Norma Millay.

Still, there were times when I did talk about Steepletop, and Millay, and Dillon. And there is the world out there, so ready, with its random and cynical moments, to give you more than you bargained for. A friend I was talking with was a writer, and not young. When I had said a little, when I had spoken George Dillon's name, he rubbed his beard and—I give you his moment of grace—looked discomfited.

In the winter of 1949 or 1950, my writer/friend said, he had been working late at night in the office of a poetry magazine, of which he was then editor. The phone rang. It was Edna Millay. She was crying, near hysteria. He thought she had been drinking. She was trying to find George Dillon.

If Hermes is the god of hope, is he not also the god of horror? For he needs such help, and we are but a motley world. My writer/friend told Millay (he told me) to pull herself together. He told her he would find Dillon and would give him the message. Then they hung up.

My writer/friend knew (he told me) that Dillon at that time was in California, on vacation. My writer/friend did not try to find him. He did not pass on the message then, or ever, and not from lassitude or passivity but from another kind of reasoning: he felt that Dillon (or, any man) had no need of such a message coming from an hysterical woman (his words), especially a woman he did not know very well, which was his assumption. So Dillon never knew about the phone call. And Millay, assuming the message had been delivered, must have made whatever one makes of expectation, and ensuing silence.

Millay died in October 1950, a cold night at Steepletop. Dillon died in 1968, at his home in South Carolina, in the shining month of May.

Someone, one day, will publish a biography of Millay, and everything will be in it that a careful and caring study can retrieve of the complex, difficult, dazzling life of another human being. It will not be definitive. It will be valuable, and as truthful as it can be. We need to be each others' storytellers—at least we have to try. One wants to know what the beautiful strangers were like—one *needs* to know. Still, it is like painting the sky. What stars have been left out, or their places mistaken, misinterpreted, not noticed at all? I think I know a lot about Millay. What does it come to, half a basket? Can anyone know enough about another life? We have to hope so. But it is a fearful task, each telling of the great tale. The night is dark. I hear the wind pacing, its dread power. I hear the phone ringing, late at night, its passionate words about to be understood, or misunderstood. I feel the heart, at the door of its body, going down the long stone stairs and out of this world, alone.

Sand Dabs, One

Lists, and verbs, will carry you many a dry mile.

To imitate or not to imitate—the question is easily satisfied. The perils of not imitating are greater than the perils of imitating.

Always remember—the speaker doesn't do it. The words do it.

Look for verbs of muscle, adjectives of exactitude.

The idea must drive the words. When the words drive the idea, it's all floss and gloss, elaboration, air bubbles, dross, pomp, frump, strumpeting.

Don't close the poem as you opened it, unless your name is Blake and you have written a poem about a Tyger.

A Few Words

Nothing in the forest is charming. Gardens are charming, and man-made grottos, and there is a tranquility about some scenes of husbandry and agriculture that is charming—orderly rows of vegetation, or lazy herds, or the stalks of harvest lashed and leaning together.

And nothing in the forest is cute. The dog fox is not cute, nor the little foxes. I watch them as they run up and down the dune. One is carrying the soiled wing of a gull; the others grab onto it and pull. They fly in and out of the blond grasses, their small teeth snapping. They are not adorable, or charming, or cute.

The owl is not cute. The milk snake is not cute, nor the spider in its web, nor the striped bass. Neither is the skunk cute, and its name is not "Flower." Nor is there a rabbit in the forest whose name is "Thumper," who is cute.

Toys are cute. But animals are not toys. Neither are trees, rivers, oceans, swamps, the Alps, the mockingbird singing all night in the bowers of thorn, the snapping turtle, or the purple-fleshed mushroom.

Such words—"cute," "charming," "adorable"—miss the mark, for what is perceived of in this way is stripped of dignity, and authority. What is cute is entertainment, and replaceable. The words lead us and we follow: what is cute is diminutive, it is powerless, it is capturable, it is trainable, it is ours. It is all a mistake. At our feet are the ferns—savage and resolute they rose, when the race of man was *nowhere* and altogether unlikely ever to be at all, in the terrifying shallows of the first unnamed and unnameable oceans. We find them pretty, delicate, and charming, and carry them home to our gardens.

Thus we manage to put ourselves in the masterly way—if nature is full of a hundred thousand things adorable and charming, diminutive and powerless, then who is in the position of power? We are! We are the parents, and the governors. The notion facilitates a view of the world as playground and laboratory, which is a meager view surely. And it is disingenuous, for it seems so harmless, so responsible. But it is neither.

For it makes impossible the other view of nature, which is of a realm both sacred and intricate, as well as powerful, of which we are no more than a single part. Nature, the total of all of us, is the wheel that drives our world; those who ride it willingly might yet catch a glimpse of a dazzling, even a spiritual restfulness, while those who are unwilling simply to hang on, who insist that the world must be piloted by man for his own benefit, will be dragged around and around all the same, gathering dust but no joy.

Humans or tigers, tigers or tiger lilies—note their differences and still how alike they are! Don't we all, a few summers, stand here, and face the sea and, with whatever physical and intellectual deftness we can muster, improve our state—and then, silently, fall back into the grass, death's green cloud? What is cute or charming as it rises, as it swoons? Life is Niagara, or nothing. I would not be the overlord of a single blade of grass, that I might be its sister. I put my face close to the lily, where it stands just above the grass, and give it a good greeting from the stem of my heart. We live, I am sure of this, in the same country, in the same household, and our burning comes from the same lamp. We are all wild, valorous, amazing. We are, none of us, cute.

The Poet's Voice

As the great cats of the world are known for speed and grace; as the black ant is known for tyranny and industry; as the yak and oxen are known for brute strength and mild temper, so mankind is known for invention. It is the trademark of our species. All mankind desires to be up and doing, and the business of the day is whatever is new. There fortune lies, and fame, and the promise of happiness. No man need be bored but may become a sort of divinity as he gathers around him the old materials, and takes them apart, and cuts and pastes them into some new arrangement, and presently gives to the world a substance transformed, a whirligig never before seen, a flower of a new color, a square egg, or a poem—a poem in which the old and the new are conjoined: the old material is dealt with with new insight, or the old instance with a fresh metaphor, or the old emotion with altered diction. And there we have it: a new creation. Such is the nature of man, by which, of course, I mean man in the species sense—I mean men and boys and women and girls. Most certainly, too, I mean children.

For each poet's voice begins in childhood—in the human instance, in the history of time and experience. That is, it begins with those poems encountered in the first instance. Beyond doubt, in order to become a doer and a maker, it is necessary first that the mind's attention be entrapped and enthralled by what already exists. In order to become a lover of poetry, and a maker of poems, it is necessary, first, to love a poem. Then, a few poems. Not from the idea of olives do we come at last to savor that Mediterranean fruit, but from one bite, and then another bite, until the assurance of felicity is bound to the category—to the concept of the fruit itself, in all its instances. We begin to learn through partaking, through experience. We learn by putting the olive into our mouths. We learn by putting the actual poem into our mouths—or, in this case, into our minds. We learn by curiosity and attention—by confrontation—then by imitation. From such experience and effort the intellect and spirit take on power, and move toward their own individuality.

Thus it is that these early experiences—these poems of first instance—are profoundly important. I mean, what poems they are, what nature is theirs, and tone, and their intent, their heft, their music, their message, their mirth, their clarity, their vocabulary, their passion—all of this is profoundly important. With these first instances, one feels and meditates upon the way language deals with the actualities of the world—one gets an immediate sense of the many things language can do, and how. In just the way that all first experiences, making their way as novel forces across the still-forming landscapes of the mind, are likely to exist through an entire lifetime as the most important, most emotive, most influential experiences of their own kind—in just this way, poems of the first influence are profound.

The first poems that I found—I mean, found by myself, on the page, and read by myself, in amazement and delight—were poems of Whitman. For this, I will never be less than deeply grateful. Here was language that was rich and choice; here was prodigious energy; here was cadence; here was the total investment of attention in a thousand directions. I understood immediately that certain things—attention, great energy, total concentration, tenderness, risk, beauty—were elements of poetry. And I understood that these elements did not grow as grass grows from a seed, naturally and unstoppably, but rather were somehow gathered or discovered by the poet, and placed inside the poem. I understood that the poem was a construct—that it required form, elegance, objectivity.

Moreover, along with the robust, the assured, the almost oracular tone was the familiar, the intimate, the companionable voice:

I teach straying from me, yet who can stray from me?
I follow you whoever you are from the present hour;
My words itch at your ears till you understand them.

An avuncular poet! Who was, at the same time, the masterly public poet, whose diction of leaping iambs, of common speech, was made lustrous in line after line through the presumption that the ordinary, described with the finest of interest, devotion, and word-craft, was no longer ordinary:

> *Where the katydid works her chromatic reed on the*
> *walnut-tree over the well;*
> *Through patches of citrons and cucumbers with silver-*
> *wired leaves . . .*

I doted upon Whitman's seriousness, his willingness to take himself lightly while taking the work of the poem seriously:

> *I do not say these things for a dollar, or to fill up the time*
> *while I wait for a boat. . . .*

> *A morning-glory at my window satisfies me more than the*
> *metaphysics of books. . . .*

Or this:

> *I think I could turn and live awhile with the animals. . . .*
> *they are so placid and self-contained,*
> *I stand and look at them sometimes half the day long.*

> *They do not sweat and whine about their condition,*
> *They do not lie awake in the dark and weep for their sins,*

They do not make me sick discussing their duty to God,
Not one is dissatisfied. . . . not one is demented with the
mania of owning things,
Not one kneels to another, nor to his kind that lived
thousands of years ago,
Not one is respectable or industrious over the whole earth.

Though Whitman was the first, and my attachment to him has remained, after a half century of his company, as intense and comfortable as it was in those first years, there were others.

There was Poe, whose swarmy meter and alliteration spilled me into a waking dream. There was Blake, whose subjects were always molten, whose cages were always four-square and gossamer. There was Whittier, there was Longfellow, there was Walter de la Mare.

The Listeners

"Is there anybody there?" said the Traveller,
    Knocking on the moonlit door;
And his horse in the silence champed the grasses
    Of the forest's ferny floor:
And a bird flew up out of the turret,
    Above the Traveller's head:
And he smote upon the door again a second time;
    "Is there anybody there?" he said.
But no one descended to the Traveller;
    No head from the leaf-fringed sill
Leaned over and looked into his grey eyes,
    Where he stood perplexed and still.

But only a host of phantom listeners
    That dwelt in the lone house then
Stood listening in the quiet of the moonlight
    To that voice from the world of men:
Stood thronging the faint moonbeams on the dark stair,
    That goes down to the empty hall,
Hearkening in an air stirred and shaken
    By the lonely Traveller's call.
And he felt in his heart their strangeness,
    Their stillness answering his cry,
While his horse moved, cropping the dark turf,
    'Neath the starred and leafy sky;
For he suddenly smote on the door, even
    Louder, and lifted his head:—
"Tell them I came, and no one answered,
    That I kept my word," he said.
Never the least stir made the listeners,
    Though every word he spake
Fell echoing through the shadowiness of the still house
    From the one man left awake:
Ay, they heard his foot upon the stirrup,
    And the sound of iron on stone,
And how the silence surged softly backward,
    When the plunging hoofs were gone.

And there was Keats, there were Shelley and
Wordsworth; there were Coleridge, and yes, Shake-
speare, Milton, and Gray; and there was Keats:

A Thing of Beauty

A thing of beauty is a joy for ever:
Its loveliness increases; it will never
Pass into nothingness; but still will keep
A bower quiet for us, and a sleep
Full of sweet dreams, and health, and quiet breathing.
Therefore, on every morrow, are we wreathing
A flowery band to bind us to the earth,
Spite of despondence, of the inhuman dearth
Of noble natures, of the gloomy days,
Of all the unhealthy and o'er-darkened ways
Made for our searching: yes, in spite of all,
Some shape of beauty moves away the pall
From our dark spirits. Such the sun, the moon,
Trees old, and young, sprouting a shady boon
For simple sheep; and such are daffodils
With the green world they live in; and clear rills
That for themselves a cooling covert make
'Gainst the hot season; the midforest brake,
Rich with a sprinkling of fair musk-rose blooms:
And such too is the grandeur of the dooms
We have imagined for the mighty dead;
All lovely tales that we have heard or read:
An endless fountain of immortal drink,
Pouring unto us from the heaven's brink.
Nor do we merely feel these essences
For one short hour; no, even as the trees
That whisper round a temple become soon
Dear as the temple's self, so does the moon,
The passion poesy, glories infinite,
Haunt us till they become a cheering light
Unto our souls, and bound to us so fast,
That, whether there be shine, or gloom o'ercast,
They always must be with us, or we die.

American poetry underwent many changes in the first half of the century, as we all know. The language of speech, primarily iambic, entered the poem. The design of the poem on the page became more varied; and this design became an important part of signifying to the reader how the poet wanted the poem read and, thus, felt. The relationship between reader and poem—now the usual scene was of a single reader reading a poem silently to himself or herself—changed too. It was becoming, one might almost say, intimate. Since diction had taken off its fancy dress and gone sauntering through the countryside, the poem had become a conversation, or a document at least as personal as a letter written by a friend and intended for a friend's reception. Sometimes the poem was even more intimate than that: it was as personal as a journal entry made by the poet for his or her own eyes; in any case we read it—and were meant to read it—as though over the writer's shoulder. In no way did the new poems present themselves to the public, in the old style, with hat and gloves, loyal to a meter and "carefulling" their speech.

Much about all of this is good. Everything about all of this is good! As an example, many of James Wright's poems (they would of course have been written before 1980), employ what might be called an intensified vernacular—a diction which is effective, interesting, tremendously moving. Such plainspoken poems were surely felt as an invitation to writers who did not get schooled in the old classical traditions.

Women writers, many of them returning to the world of artistic endeavor after raising families—Afro-American writers, Native American writers—they all had a more likely entrance into the world of the poem with examples of such an accessible diction before them, and the participation of such ethnic and cultural groups has, there is no doubt about it, enriched our literature beyond measure.

Corresponding changes were going on as well with subject matter. Unlocked forever were the gates outside which the uninvited subjects of poems were tossing their pretty heads, and their not-so-pretty heads. We no longer talk about what subject matter is appropriate and what is not so appropriate. It is all appropriate.

And, still, I feel myself so fortunate to have come along when I did, in time to gather as poems of initial influence the incantations of Keats, and the mossy twilights of de la Mare, and that muscular riddle the endless "I" of Whitman, with his pensive "exuberations." I look now to the differences, as I see them, between such poems and the more contemporary work, that might have been my initial influence but was not, to discover why.

In the first place, there is the question of meter. For the present generation, it has become such an apparatus of the past that youngsters—even college students—who had no early dealings with Mother Goose, or poems such as the Keats or the de la Mare,

are not even susceptible to its enhancements. It is not, for them, the loom upon which pattern and pattern-pleasure are built; it is, rather, a burden and an obstacle. Many are the young writers who read the old poems wholly for content; the poem's prosody does not, in the privacy of the reading mind, from the printed page, spring into shaking and passionate life.

My meaning is not to disparage the conversational stride of the modern poem. But can we have anything but concern for the young writer who is shut away from those palaces of pleasure, the old rhythms? Moreover, is it not proper to remember that the free-verse poem was thought of, thought about, and first written by writers deeply sensitive to poems of meter and rhyme? Such poets were able to cast out what they wished not to keep, and to harbor what they did not wish lost. Notice, for a while, how many final phrases in free-verse poems conclude with one or two dactyls, then one or two strong stresses—the architecture of meter is still a vital part of the poem.

It was good fortune for me, I'm sure of it, that I was first presented poems of rhythm and meter—the old grandfathers of the nineteenth century and earlier. Thus, in the nature of things, I recognized free verse, when I came to it, not as opponent to but as deriving from the old poems—a far more interesting and fruitful way to consider free verse than simply to come upon it as a design which is rhythmless and meterless. Why is this so? I think most of all because the writer who considers poems of meter and free-verse poems as *associates* will not hesitate to let things blend a little, knowing that the boundaries are not bristling and straight, but are friendly, even pliant. The free-verse poem may want, here and there, to whisper in the old, wild, metered way—so, why not? Moreover, having heard meter—with the inner ear, I mean—a writer is naturally more likely (than a nonlistener) to be able to use it, even occasionally, with skill.

Along with the alteration of the design of the poem have come, as I have said, substantial changes in the poem's diction and its subject matter. Much was gained by these changes, but certain things were lost. There was, in the tone of the old poems, a certainty, an authority which was implied and fortified through its elevated diction. Of course I am not talking about poetic diction! I am talking about a diction and a tone that was *other* than the daily, the usual, the ordinary. In and of itself, apart from the content of the poem, this tone suggested to the reader that something of import was on the page—was contained within the occasion of the poem. Since, as I see it, the work of the poem is to transcend the ordinary instance, to establish itself on a second, metaphysical level, this tone was important, and useful. It served, in the old poem, as a steeple serves a church; even in the distance it says: Here is holy ground. Here is something different from everyday.

There is also the actual landscape of the poem. Many of the old poems take place in a world different from—other than—the usual one. They take place in a world that exists nowhere but in the meeting between the words and the reader's imagination. It is a world in which the strictures of earthly time and space have not been drawn. Stories, usually, operate through the familiar laws of cause and effect; and they happen, say, between three-thirty and four-thirty P.M. on Main Street, in some named town. Now, in the world of the new poem, which is so likely to be a world ordinary and familiar, the poem is also likely to take place on Main Street, and at a certain hour. And again, much is gained; much is lost.

The frequent reminder of, and the wide entrance into, the other world—the world of fancy and myth, of pure imagination—has to a great extent been lost, or if not lost then reduced, made small and improbable. The old poems so willingly presented the most unlikely fancies or narratives! The lovely fairy-tale otherworldly quality of "The Listeners," with its shrouded and then released emotion—its mystery an essential part of this emotion—released me in 1950, and releases me today, from *this* world. And this release is, I suggest, one of the primary charges of creative work. For unless we are released from this world we cannot enter the magical, the heroic, the imaginary existence. We cannot stand up in willing bondage to the priorities of any other world than the material, actual one.

The actual world! The important contemporary work in poetry is work in which the actualities of life are the important news, the important landscapes. It is work worth celebrating. And yet I miss those poems that opened mysterious and shimmering doors so easily into another world. Poems like "Endymion," "Christabel," "Annabel Lee," whose fabric existed nowhere but in the imagination and which, because reading them was a felt experience, verified for me in those first confrontations the power of imagination— the capability of imagination—the immense and unchallengeable *reality* of imagination.

But the most important change, as I see it, is the change in the poem's intent, which is expressed by the persona of the poem. The "I" of the poem. Most simply put, the "I" of the contemporary poem is rather likely to be a reflection of the author of the poem. Anyway, there is no large error made, no insult intended, when one assumes this to be so. I did not, however, ever make such a presumption about the "I" of poems during my youthful reading, and I think that what I did assume is closer to the intent of poetry altogether.

The "I" of the old poem, I assumed, was not at all a "knowable" person, a person much like myself. It was at once two other, and more important things. First, it was an "I" wrapped in the mystery of the poem, and the authority of the poem's diction. It was elevated by the poetic forces within the poem and, at least for the length of the poem, it was infallible. And it was, even more importantly, a conduit between myself, and the divine timelessness of the poem. If it was really Shelley who stood and listened to the skylark, it was not Shelley in any important sense; he did not mean for me, reading the poem, to be thinking about him listening to the bird; he was entirely willing to vanish, and to let *me* become the "I." I am sure of it, he knew that both things were necessary—that he vanish, and that the reader enter the poem. Indeed, I took it to be my task to enter the poem, to become the speaker of the poem, to reenact the poem as if I were the experiencer. The poem was never invested with the author's personal history in a way that meant to keep the reader from this kind of participation—in any way that would allow the reader *only* the role of reader. Simply put, poems, I thought, were not about authors. They were about me. And they were not about stasis, they were about experience, and passage.

And, so, *I* was the horseman in "The Listeners." I looked at the animals in the field "half the day long." It was I who contemplated time, and a thing of beauty. And this is what I came to believe: it was the purpose of the poem to give the reader an arrangement of words in which an experience or an insight waited to be felt through, and I mean in an individual and personal way. Only thus could the poem make an indelible mark upon the reader. Only thus could the poem become an abiding part of the reader's own life. A reader would enter the poem—let us assume with a supple wit and a whole heart—and would emerge a little different, forever, from what he or she had been before.

No poem is about one of us, or some of us, but is about all of us. It is part of a long document about the species. Every poem is about my life but also it is about your life, and a hundred thousand lives to come. That one person wrote it is not nearly so important or so interesting as that it pertains to us all.

And, in fact, that one person did write the poem is arguable. Certainly one person sat down with pen and paper, or with computer as the case may be, and put down the sense of it and the design of it. But such gestures are only the final actions in a long series of necessary procedures. For the poet—as all workers in all artistic disciplines and in all professions—proceeds to the work through education, through trial and correction and advisement, through imitation, through the influence of the ten thousand things that surround any inquisitive mind. Each of us brings to the poem, to the moving pen, a world of echoes.

Also, for the poet as well as anyone else, each day in the private realm is filled with its mundane details, its noise, its flutterings, its passions, amusements, trips to the grocery store, to the mall for socks, to the car wash, to the ball game. Such activities however are surface activities—the curl up and the breakage of waves. And poems do not come from that part of the ocean; they come from the dark and heavy and portentous and almost impenetrable depths. This is where the poem erupts and begins to shape itself. It is also the place where the poem matters, where it is read—for this place exists in every human mind whether one is a writer or not. Each of us, in our lives, opens to this deep place at moments of ceremony, of crisis, of passage, and of transcendence, at moments of terror and at moments of great joy. It is where some understanding about our lives is sought, even if it is not always found.

A good portion of our lives is gladly casual, and happily ordinary. This other dark and lustrous place is not casual. It is not ordinary. Neither does it pertain so much to the particularities of our lives as to the commonality of our lives. The voice that speaks from this place is not the voice of a person of such and such an age, such and such a race, such and such a social security number. Jung is talking about this place when he talks about the collective unconscious; Eliot was talking about it when he suggested that through poems we can escape individual personality. The diver must wear a mask to live; the writer must wear a mask in order to be something, or someone, other than himself. In such a mask, the writer goes down, into the ocean, under its luminous tonnage, and through, and out from the levels of the personal life.

Therefore whatever the diver takes with him—and the diver without equipment is soon a drowned diver—is of immeasurable importance. I will pass over such necessities as a modest attitude, technical adroitness, language skills altogether. These of course are as essential as the oxygen a diver must carry with him.

Something else that the poet, that diver, takes with him down into the fathoms of the workplace is an abiding and previously thought-out sense of what a poem is, of what its *purpose* is. Which sense we put together through our own reflections based, first of all, upon the impression we receive from examples we have before us—especially, I think, from those mighty *first* examples. We react, we imitate, we imagine, we invent.

And now I have come full circle, back to those poems of first instance, to talk again of their inescapably important role in a writer's sense of what art is—and their inescapably important role in the cast and tenor of my own poetic voice.

A few years ago, in an interview, I said: when I am doing my job well, I vanish. I mean this, thoroughly. And certainly this intention—for it is by intention that I vanish—is different from the intention of poems behind which there exists a strong and definite poet-person. Such poems have emerged, mostly, from the so-called "confessional" school. Many are the ways to behold the blackbird, and many are the ways to consider the value of a poem, but for myself, as surely is plain now, the way of reenactment is the way into the valuable core of the poem. Poems which do not allow this do not serve me in the way that I want poems to serve me.

Which is to say that I look to be served by poems. I look for them to be ongoing presences within my life, not interludes—not places apart. And I look for them to be vital and informative and affirming—affirming "reenactment/experiences" enlarging my life. They need not always be graceful, or wise, or simple. Like life itself, they may well contain terror and pain and confusion, but they need to strive on behalf of the lord of life and not the lesser gods of self-interest, of havoc, of death. They need to be poems of passage, not of stasis.

Confessional poetry is not my subject here, and is not at all so simple a subject that it can be dealt with quickly. Yet a few remarks are called for. Poems of the confessional school—whose "I" voices are the authors' voices and so intended, and whose texts are so often aggrieved and aggressive, frantic and self-involved— seem to me more catharsis than art, more memoir than poem. I turn from them having learned a little about the authors perhaps, but nothing at all about the world beyond personal frenzy, the huge energies it can produce, the darkness it can long for, the anguish and anger that can pour forth from it, like rain. In a hundred years I suspect such poems will be seen as a derivative of therapy, that exercise in which the "I" is encouraged to become, as once indeed in infancy it felt itself to be, the center of the world.

And yet such poems can and often do demonstrate enormous skill, and within their frantic pages human suffering and human courage is plain to see. I think it quite possible that their fabric of rent privacy, of pain and frustration, is one of the elements that played an important role in preparing the climate in which the more recent school of poetry has blossomed, producing poems in which private life, personal experience is used by persons from many ethnic or cultural backgrounds. But, in these cases the stories are told for a clear purpose—to reveal something of a previously ignored part of humanity, to reveal injustice, to inform and thus move, and therefore to excite change. In such poems the subject is never the poet only, or the poet's life only; rather the personal experience is presented as part of history, and part of the present—the present that could bend like hot glass, should the human heart at last listen—should the human reader enter the poem and understand, through the experience of the poem, what it has not understood before. The work of art is, as we know, available to all—to the well and to the ill. Paintings by psychotic patients, with their terrible dance upon the canvas, are often enough stunning. But it takes health—and health takes release from the crushing fist of self-concern—for poems to escape their own creator and genesis and belong to the world of shining and useful things.

What about my own experiences? Do they, or any part of them, become poems? Maybe. Sometimes. More or less. Such experiences, however, are not the point. They may be the material. But they waver, they adjust, they even lie, for the sake of something else. For they know that the poem intends to rise from its own singularity, its own instance, which is relatively unimportant, to a less particular, though just as exacting, conceptual level. Poems must employ language to illustrate *idea,* that sacred smoke above the fire of instance. And the "I" of the poem must gesture to the threshold, in invitation.

A final thought, but perhaps the most interesting of all. The voice in which the poet works, whatever it is—cherished and molded and polished over the years—is, as any voice is, indicative of an attitude, a sensibility—almost, one might say, of an *other.* Any working poet lives in the company of this other, and in an intense relationship. A working poet in fact very likely hears this voice more than he or she hears any other voice. And any working poet is, therefore, likely to be drawn to those influences, activities, and thoughts that will stimulate, please, and enliven this inner companion/voice. Do you see what I am saying? The voice which a poet forms is not any more something that a poet creates than it is something, over the years, that creates the poet. Throughout my life, unquestionably, I have made decisions one way or another based on the influence of this inner voice—this authority with which I most intensely and willingly live.

There is a poem by Rilke—many of you know it, I am sure—that expresses a great deal of what I have been trying to say here. It is a poem about beauty. It says what I have believed all my life, and what I have tried to make my own poems mean, and greatly through the authority and challenge of voice. If beauty in general and the beautiful poem in particular does not mean something—if it does not charge us with a difficult and ennobling task—then what can beauty be after all but utter madness? But beauty is not madness—it is the challenge to be sane, to be thoughtful, to be wholesome.

This is the poem.

Archaic Torso of Apollo

We have no idea what his fantastic head
was like, where the eyeballs were slowly swelling. But
his body now is glowing like a lamp
whose inner eyes, only turned down a little,

hold their flame, shine. If there weren't light, the curve
of the breast wouldn't blind you, and in the swerve
of the thighs a smile wouldn't keep on going
toward the place where the seeds are.

If there weren't light, this stone would look cut off
where it drops so clearly from the shoulders,
its skin wouldn't gleam like the fur of a wild animal,

and the body wouldn't send out light from every edge
as a star does . . . for there is no place at all
that isn't looking at you. You must change your life.

Sand Dabs, Two

The sound of a dog splashing about in the creek. Not like a boy, not like a fish, but like Ben, precisely.

I am mad, as the saying goes, for the music of Schumann and Wolf.

The shriek, then the happiness of the drawn nail. How it blinks again, in the sunlight.

The world spins, doesn't it? Change rules the universe, doesn't it?

There's life and there's opera, and I want both.

Ben, circling through the fields. He has a whole university in his nose.

The Shelleys. They lived in the burn of ideals. They lived with awful fate lurking.

The spider: out of the sink, into the geraniums. Then I forget and water the geraniums vigorously.

Why not believe in the goldfinches. The thistles, too.

While I watched, the fly went into Ben's snapping mouth, then, out again. Then, in.

Afterword

Writing this book has been like bathing the dog—with every go-around it has come out a little cleaner. Still, there's a time when the dog is in danger of becoming too clean, and losing his dogginess altogether. Just so, in similar fear of washing too much away—for I hope some bits of the actual world, chaff and grit, will cling to these pages—I put down the towel and call the book done.

Books carry with them the bias, the enthusiasms, and, too, the faults of their authors. This book is biased, opinionated; also it is joyful, and probably there's despair here too—can a life slide forward sixty years without it? But the reader will find the pleasures more certain, and more constant, than the rills of despond; thus it has turned out in my life so far, influenced by the sustaining passions: love of the wild world, love of literature, love for and from another person.

It is dark now, not the first curve of night but the last curve: my hour. The light will soon rise out of this necessary dark. I go to my work, as I like to call it, being whimsical and serious at once. That is, to walk, and look at things, and listen, and to write down words in a small notebook. Later on, a long time later, a gathering of these words may become something I will think worth risking between the boards of another book, so you may know—if, as I hope, this one has made you more curious about the wild world than you were previously—just what I saw or heard this hour in the sweet darkness.

Perhaps.

In the meantime, good night.

Publication Acknowledgments

My thanks to the editors of the periodicals in which the following essays first appeared, sometimes in slightly different form:

"Pen and Paper and a Breath of Air": *Seneca Review* special issue titled *Taking Note: From Poets' Notebooks* (Fall 1991)

"My Friend Walt Whitman": *The Massachusetts Review* (Spring 1992)

"Four Companions with a Zest for Life": *The Boston Globe* (May 24, 1992)

"Owls": *Orion* (Spring 1995)

"Blue Pastures": *DoubleTake* (Spring 1995)

I am indebted to Molly Malone Cook, who, while working on an entirely different venture in the Special Collections Room of the Alderman Library at the University of Virginia Library, found and brought home copies of the letters of Millay and Dillon and other unpublished papers to which I make reference in the essay "Steepletop."

I wish to express my gratitude also to Nan Sherman Sussmann, for allowing me to use the five lines from George Dillon's poem "Anatomy of Death," and to Robert Bly for his translation of the sonnet by Rainer Maria Rilke, which he has titled "Archaic Torso of Apollo."